GIGGLE FOR THE TWEEPLE

TABLE OF CONTENTS

WHAT AN ES
THE CHIRP?

What is the Chirp? All right, where you have been.. Laughing out loud? The chirp would have to be the fastest taxi stand of growth in Internet today. Take the internet by storm and there are about 10.000 new users in the daytime getting ready to take part in this revolution of the internet.

The chirp is more convenient described like a bus taking its personal daily newspaper in the Internet platform. You are limited to 140 characters every time that you make a bringing up to date, which one initially, a little bit can seem. However, like you he becomes converted in more experienced, what you can accommodate in 140 characters simply is amazing.

That said, the Chirp is a lot, a lot more than that. It is like an enormous global room of conference, but anyway, he does not have to be. It all depends how many people that you follow on the Chirp. If you are in the thousands, back then your Tweet-stream will flow quickly and as you louse up what you enter for chocolate with all. If you only obey several hundred, or even less, back then things are too further easy to maintain up with.

The chirp is also a great form to meet the new on-line people, in particular those with similar interests for you. I will show you how to do this more like we thorugh of progress this report.

HOW ESTABLISHING ONESELF

Establishing oneself on the Chirp to have yours to
keep the accounts it is easy, but there are some things
of which you should be in the know when organizing
your account. This can have application software even
if you right now make an existent account also, that
way to consider these pieces of advice and that can
get better your experience informs Twittter.

The first thing to make if you do not have an account you
are the push for which http://www.twitter.com/es the
home page of Gorjeo. You will be asked for either the log
on or the record. If you do not have an account, then of
course you will need getting registered. So we experience
the process of registration and let's shuffle it all here.

REGISTRATION

Gorjeo's screen will require its Christian name and last name
and then this will make a revision it is at the one you entered
in correctly. An unripe ticktock will appear next to the box.
The following box requires you an user name and this is where
you need to give some thought stops how you are going to
imagine yourself on the Chirp. You should remember you
can establish yourself more than an account on the Chirp,
but you will need a different email address for each one.
Now this is where the thinking small piece enters. The first
account that you register always should be in its name if you
can have it. Serve yourself, the common nouns like JohnSmith
(there are no spaces in names of user) right now he will be
cheated. No matter how it is pertinent to bring variations on
his name like John Smith, or John Smith23 or any variation
tastes that. You only can use a line drawn beneath a word
in an user name. The dashes are not allowed at the field.
It is not absolutely critical that you register your name,
but you would suggest that you make if you can, in
particular if your name is unusual one. I am sure the last
thing that you want is somebody else impersonating
him on the Chirp, or anywhere else for that matter.
If you have the desire to register a business name, back then you
can do that of course, but can make him his to use your name in
the sign above the process that way is that you are identifiable
to you and connected under the name of the company you get
registered. The concepts and the reasons to operate below
each kind of registration will argue themselves later.
You are now asked of your email address. Email addresses
are associated to accounts and you only will be able to
use your email address once. For each account that you
register, you will need a different email address.
The last thing to make is refilling toggle joint to the
Captcha and back then click in Create My Cuenta.

The following screen will ask if you want to add to any of your friends of the popular plot that the based e-mail programs. You can make that later if you desire.

The following screen shows an internal telephone directory of people that the Chirp asks you if you would like to understand. Choose a certain amount if you like, but I would not get upset. I prefer to find my friends on the Chirp. When you click on Finishing, you then will be taken to your Gorjeo's account very own. You are put in journal inside and in good condition to go!

HIS ADJUSTMENTS

The following thing that we are going to make is
complementing our adjustments and this has a lot of
importance on the Chirp. You will find access ad hoc on the top
superior good of the screen, room he will couple left-wing.
They are some costs through the top in this page
that you will see you there. We will concentrate
on account's label for the moment.
The information that you entered associating is right now
entered in here, but now is time to pad this go of that way
it is that you can find people for him on the Chirp and you
also make him an interesting person to be continuous
by yourself. People will use the information you enter in
here to do that decision, but very of what you are so that
one entered you are also searchable on the Chirp and the
application softwares third various direct of party.
A thing to notice is that you can change your user name
at any time in this screen. You only have to enter your
password to do that. Although he can become, you can
disorder your follower's base, so you would not put in
a good word for him to make it on a weekly base.
Above all change your time zone for yours and
then move on the only line bioh.
Your Bio

You have 160 characters here to sell. Take some time on that
and be good for him. Simply do not enter a lot of key words
as they seem to be completely uninteresting to populate,
although they can find you. Use key words by all means, but let
out his Bio with the words that I am and then himself I describe.
So you would be able to lay eggs for example:-

I am an excursionist and smart gardener that also has a passion for the open, internet commercializing and the affiliate commercializing who also is in love for social means of communication.

Now that the description is only 143 characters, so you still something would be able to have more than key words in the bio. You can without a doubt see them that are there which one is the gardener, excursionist, internet commercializing, affiliated commercializing and them social means of communication. Using these terms inside your bio will have you to happen in the results of search when people walk looking for that another one as disposed individuals keep on. As you can see, you are worthy of taking time to understand the bio correctly.

The Balance of Screen

Introduce your name of the taxi stand Web or keep your own personal diary in the Internet here if you have one. Make sure that you include the prefix of HTTP: To the address. Your location is her following and you are also important that way it is that people can search and they can find the other ones in their same area. You will also be important for you if you chase rankings on the Chirp like the users infect with plague for your locations.

Protect Bringing Ups To Date

This is included if you want to have a private account and you have to approve the followers. NEVER light this if you mean to use Chirp to meet new people. Only they would not be able to be suffering from a cold asking for permission to follow you unless they know you personally.
You now can save your adjustments, but can rear here on that there is also a link to suppress your account if you occasionally have the desire to do that.

DEVICES

You can get into your motive telephone number here if you want bringing ups to date of Gorjeo for your telephone. Personally, I can think not about any worse thing, in particular if you have a couple of thousand followers.

ADS

You can make I Chirp nudging a text for your motive if
you have not updated in 24 hours. How annoying!
Respuestas's show is interesting one and will determine
what cheeps that you see that you are so that a prefix with
the symbol got. This is how you direct one pious for a
particular individual. There is a great explanation of the
help screen in this, so you push there to do his decision.
The rest of ads are explanatory ego. It is worthy of seeing that
a little bit of explanation possibly needs the Direct Messages
however so that it is referred to that. If you understand
somebody and they go after you, the Direct Messages can
be sent that you will not appear in Gorjeo's timeline. They
are messages unconscious between two people. If you
are Gorjeo's infrequent user, it can be worth the while to
switch on the electricity receiving notifications by email
that way it is that you can respond. In another way omit it
as only you will fill your mailbox with more disorder.

In like manner, the notifications that you have only a new
follower your e-mail enlarges them and I would leave you
completely unless to you the bourdonnement of being
said that somebody new has followed you likes it.

THE PICTURE'S LABEL

This is important really. When you open this page you will see the small avatar on screen that it is the default for the Chirp. If you love the new followers, putting your photo per se here is imperative. If you run Gorjeo's account for your company or business, back then your logo is ideal. But only put something like that it is that you can be identified in the Tweetstream by your followers. The graphic is often more important than your name when people examine Tweets with a CAT scanner and you will stand out for yours.

THE DESIGN'S LABEL

You can change the track record of your page
of Gorjeo of the default here.

The chirp arranges than a number of alternatives you can
make a selection or you the TV is able to send its track
record. You can also change all the colors if you desire.
Again, whatever you make, only you change it that way
you do not run the default. You come out to light that you
have taken quite a while establishing your account.
A note here it is that with the plethora of application
softwares of Gorjeo's lover out there worth mentioning,
many people not yet look at their page of plot anymore.
Still, it is one of his presence's components on the Chirp
and earn the grief becoming well. More afternoon of
you will show him locations where they can offer you
a more professional track record than those here.
All right, that is for the plan. The last thing to make now is
clicking on home page at the top of the screen and sending to
your first Tweet. Something as well as, Quiubo, I have recently
joined The Chirp instead of him and I am looking forward
to Meet the interesting people one is good early sending.
Simply introduce and click on Actualización's button.

THE CHIRP THE APPLICATION SOFTWARES OF THE LOVER

The biggest headache with the standard application software of plot of Gorjeo is that you have to hold an eagle eye on your answers and the Direct Messages like you only see the main Tweetstream on screen. Also it is banked in regards to the fact that only he exhibits about the last 20 pious, that way than if you he wants to see the elders, you he has to support himself back's pages going. That way what to make?

Piano, the unloading Tweetdeck of http://www.tweetdeck.com The first thing than you probably he will notice it is than you he will need to change the adjustments like the default it is white text in a black screen. You make it difficult to read I have found, but each for their own. Tweetdeck is brilliant in regards to the fact that the screen exhibits everything in the only to the Tweetstream, its answers and its direct messages. The columns of message have provisions 500 cheep like a default, that way scrolling down the image you let him a tight form or searching then head back they cheep that you can want to refer of return to. The screen has a correct continuous wad by the hand, so you can establish different groups and his they cheep you will appear in that column. You a so-called group would be able to have better friends and other for gardeners for example. Over there you do not guess right badly important pious of people that they are more important for you than other ones. At the moment of writing, Tweetdeck is probably the greater part of widely-used application software for the Chirp and I would highly recommend it to you.

YOUR PÍA

Begin to bring some you cheep in the system now. In the
home page Twitter, question That You Are Doing. Very
frankly they do not care about many people until you have
done their relation as a result of understanding. But there are
some good forms to begin. Continue to be that some blogs
in which you are interested by means of a RSS feed a reader
of the fodder like Google. (look for these in Google if you are
not familiar with the terms. There are piles of information
in there and you would be able to occupy an electronic book
of his.) Start by throwing the mail lace for interesting poles
on the Chirp about them with a link for the blog's pole. For
example: "Being interesting to him pole on the pest control
in tomatos. Connect ". Make sure that you always include
HTTP: / In the link and no in simply the WWW that way is that
the link is able to do click in the Tweetstream. If it is a long
link, Tweetdeck has a facility to shorten it for a small URL.
Another good shape of undertaking to cheep is with
appointments. Do a search for some appointments of concern
and cheep these. The some staffs of development are great
and also you give an appointment for famous people. There is
one that I have just to find in the Tweetstream as an example
here: " we are what repeatedly we make. Excellence, then,
is not an act, but a habit ". – Aristóteles. There is thousand
of these throughout the internet that you can use.
Whatever you do, in no the stage of your sales that lay eggs to
the current beginning Twitter and career pious after the sales
cheeps. Your race will be shortlived if you make and people
him desseguirán very quickly. The chirp is over commitment,
value and a social experience. A constant flow of links of
sales is not fair do not advance. The pole couples for its
products or its taxi stands throughout the way, but maintain

them for about 5 % of your total you cheep at the most.
Another good idea with his to cheep is holding religion
and policy set apart of them. These themes only they
can blow the followers and you can lose them.

ANSWERS

You can answer Tweet simply putting into the symbol to somebody foremost of your name. This makes cheeps to it job go for them as you appear in your column of answer or his page in place of in the general Tweet stream. It is an useful form of starting conversations with people to build accounts. Simply comment on one of his cheep. Tweetdeck has a characteristic when you the symbol right into the area of publication gravitates on the avatar of the user to put its name and reply.

RETWEETING

People give value to themselves re-pious and it is a good way
getting seen by other ones. All that you make is job RT in
front of the user name. Using Tweetdeck, flutter on the user's
avatar and absolutely everything will put that into the area of
publication. Separate his cheep of his comment if you he has
one. Usually I put two pipes, which holds down the shift key
on the character. This will produce which one clearly shows
another pious person's end and his answer or makes comments.
If other people repían his cheep, make it a habit to
habit them. It is common courtesy. Simply cheeps
user's name Thank You For RT:-) And send.

THE BIG DECISION

You are probably time now to do a big decision as you will affect the form which you use Chirp in considerably. That decision relates with quality versus quantity. If you are involved in marketing, back then followers' quantity will be important for you. You are like building a list. But if you want to walk off with personal things, back then followers' quality will be what you need. One way or another, you will have to find the following step to some people to keep on.

WINNING ADEPTS

You need first being aware that to rush out and going after a lot of people they can make you look alike to Gorjeo's potential spammer. Build his following base slowly. As time keeps on, if you chased quantity, then you will be able to add more at the same time, but would initially suggest that you get attached to 50 to begin with. The reason is ad hoc that when you go after people, more probably they will obey back. Many people do not make this automatically, although some make, in particular in the marketing space of the internet. Some people will actually go and will look at your home page of Gorjeo to make a decision if you are worthy of understanding or no in your eyes. This is where your profile and the adjustments than you took long everything the problem in making will resist all the way to you in good place.

ANY GOOD PEOPLE TO BEGIN WITH

Here there are some people you can begin to simply after of directly go. They are included because Gorjeo's exponents are big and you will learn plenty of simply observing his cheep. You will see your style of using Chirp and will be able to emulate the good points and will be able to omit what you does not like in developing your style. All of them will follow you back too much usually, so you will build your follower's base. All these people have the follower's big bases that they have built being active, linking and deciding they appreciate for the other ones on the Chirp.

Ange Recchia also known as angesbiz

Ange Recchia here best known as angesbiz on the Chirp and many another one

The Social Gathering Gets Connected. I am some Sociales Means Of Communication and adviser coach of SEO for WebVision2020 Pty Ltd and I write about Gorjeo in Http://socialnetworkingnewsdaily.com/http://socetworkingnewsdaily.com aboutThat also the love to write about Personal Desarrollo in http://angesbiz.cohttp://angesbiz.com/mhttp://angesbiz.com http://angesbiz.com/Yhttp://angesbiz.com/ou should follow me because he is on the most incredible journey of my life for the moment, is desirable to me to collide with new tweeps and he splits links that are been interested in when embark in conversation. In other words, I like to be Tertulia!

Go after Ange in http://twitter.com/angesbiz

Ric Raftis Also Known As RicRaftis

I am a Designer of the Commercial, Coach of the Internet and Affiliate of the Marketer that is in love with Gorjeo and Joomla and of Web. I am also a Cagora Community Partner in 5 Worlds. I am also a Socially Unfit Person! Follow me and I will understand back. Hire me and I will answer. I like to meet the new people and to make the new friends and the Chirp is a great form to make it. Also I run than the Maid Por taxi stand of Gorjeo in where http://www.helpviatwitter.com/que you he can obtain answer to all kind of questions on the set where you he is not restrained for 140 characters's questions.
Go after Ric in http://twitter.com/ricraftis

Mike Wesely Also Known As Mike Wesely

Hello, sure I wait for ur having a Twonderful Day. The Smart People for the most part Understand

I!!! If You are it not, You probably Would Not Like It I Anyway. As well, if your Punzada, you should go to and should observe, http://twittalk.tv go we taught the people how to use chirp more efficaciously. Check the shows Achieved in the background. If You for some reason get bored there, Cheer Up your day for to.http://videoptin.com in progress Oh but most of all, greet me using the Mike Wesely at the beginning of your pole. I always try to respond. The respectful form is that one:-)
Go after Mike in http://twitter.com/Mike Wesely http://twitter.com/Mike Wesely

Michele Price Also Known As ProsperityGal

Twucess twith http://www.blogtalkradio.com/TwitterToday, http://www.blogtalkradio.com/TwitterToday that you learn reproachful piece of advice and we introduced Tweeps every week, who you are and what you make that way is that you can build a loud networking well. I am a commercial felt woman that shows him forms given as a present to associating and she has success, oh I cook an average roasted meat also, giggle. You quote the love of the postscript to cheep inspirational to put

thinking in a focus that he requires where you want to BE.
Go after Michele in http://twitter.com/prosperitygal

Wayne Mansfield Also Known As WayneMansfield

I have come late to the Gorjeo behind long years like a Marketer Of The Internet. My business is the staging of seminaries in Australia, NZ, India and the Middle East on the commercial and personal education. The chirp is not someting ... is a level of commitment on the Chirp that allows to the meeting new people. In order to have the best of Gorjeo, I always follow you back and bracket of the I on purpose for your messages. Fun is Gorjeo and you will see the betyween in fun per se and many people. The authentic friendship makes for itself on the Chirp. Retweeting is the last compliment for the poles of other big appointments it is vitamins for the brain - when you RT than you he shares inhaling express -....Re-skewbald good pious all the time and I enjoy a good appointment or two . You make sure you say hello that way it is that we can become acquainted.
Go after Wayne in http://www.twitter.com/waynemansfield

Ivy Clark Also Known As IvyClark

I am a plot that is self-employed generalist (the designer's information developer of plot the architect) impassioned about usable design of plot and I speculate that I am geeky as I am in love with new toys. My pastimes are varied at the mercy of my state of mind - working at kitchen garden, nature walks, jewelry store making, scrapbooking, gliding over Internet, praying or only enjoying the heat in the sun. I am still relatively new for Perth, being me moved here simply he does 6 months, so really I enjoy the new thing and the excitation that everything brings of Singapore. I am in love to tap into love and like-minded people how we can share ideas, knowledge and we can learn from everybody we related to each other with in the Chirp.
Go after Ivy in http://twitter.com/ivyclark

All right, that should get you going with some people and is a good cross section there of people and styles.

TWELLOW

Twellow, in is http://www.twellow.com/otra great

way of finding people to interact to you. People here

are categorized in all the different areas and you he can

go after those with similar interests for yours.

The main page shows you all categories, the fact that then
you have takes the role like substitute categories also. You
only do click on a category and people's list in that area is
displayed.You do not have to be registered with Twellow to
be exhibited, but at the moment of writing there if people
were two million grouper's appearing of on the premises,
so you will have enough enter that electing. For everything
you want to say however, enroll to yourself and establish
a profile that way it is that the other ones can find you.
When you Twellow clicks on a category, display on
screens they have people's list in regards to the fact that
category and they are ordered to by followers' number. If
you it is right now put at journal in the Chirp by Internet,
(no Tweetdeck), you he will be able to go after people
directly of the screens where reviews are exhibited.

Mr. Cheeps

The Mister T http://www.mrtweet.net/is you form other of
obtaining benefits new followers. All that you have to make
is going after the Señor Tweet on the Chirp and his cheep
with which envelopes for contents were walked will be and

back then you he will obtain a Direct Message of him. You
then go to the taxi stand and the log on and you will obtain
proposed people's list. You will also bring people's list that
they understand you that you do not follow that way are
that you then can follow them if you make a choice.
It is one in reality I lay siege to smart child
and worth getting registered in.

LEVELER

The leveler lies on the Gorjeo like @ghttp://twitter.grader.com
http://twitter.grader.com/and be a taxi stand of some
interest. As you pawn the road on the Chirp, you can arrive
Ordered for status for Nivelador on a punctuation out
of 100. He is based on some secret algorithm apparently
that way it is than people the system cannot play.
Apart from that Nivelador's aspect, you can look straight
in the face who the outstanding Tweeple is in a particular
area or even for the theme using the show of search.
When you use the show of search, you will enroll the Tweeple
for your punctuation decreasing order. For example, if you
go after gardening in Nivelador, you will interest a list of
everybody 100 good grades in working at kitchen garden on
the Chirp. You can see your Gorjeo's bio of your account and
if you click on your Leveler's partiture, you will take him to
your Gorjeo's account from where you can follow them.
Serve yourself, you right now should be put in
journal inside for Darse A Shimmering Intonation
by yourself to follow somebody.

PIECES OF ADVICE GOTTEN AHEAD OF THAT YOU CHEEP

Now that you are on up, let's delve into some advanced pieces of advice Tweeting and application softwares that they can really encourage their Gorjeo's use up.

MAKE THE TRACK RECORDS TREMULOUS

We exchanged views earlier about establishing your track record of Gorjeo in order that only we did not seem the page predetermined of Gorjeo. Leaving that like that you show a lack of caution in his part. You need to stand out from the crowd and that attracts more followers, or at the very least prints to the people with your professionalism. Now if you are a little bit of a buzz Photoshop, back then you can make your track record, grocery store of extra features added to a program to enhance its funcionality and can charge it to your Gorjeo's profile. But if you are it not, or you only want to save time, then there are some taxi stands out there that they will make themselves for you auto-magicly. In order to find these taxi stands, the best is for simply Google track records of chirp and you will find many taxi stands offering this service free. My personalhttp://www.twitbacks.com http://www.twitbacks.com/where than you he can bring some big track records.

However, that said, if you want to do what you are due playing the violin in Photoshop, you can bring http://www.twitterbacks.com to some greathttp://www.twitterbacks.com

SOCIALTOO

SocialToo in is http://www.socialtoo.com/una
tool automatized usefully for the Chirp.

In Tertulia También, you can establish your account to
make some things of the automatic pilot for you.

Above all, you can make SocialToo fall into a trap
stops automatically following everybody that follows
you. This can remove the difficult kind of work of
checking you all his new followers and then going
and adding them to your list to reciprocate.
You can also make SocialToo fall into a trap to send a
Direct automatic Message to people that they follow you.
Don't! The Direct automatic messages are absolutely hated
over there the greater part of the Gorjeo's community,
in particular they experimented to the users because
they can choose them a mile away. It is a sterile and rude
form of undertaking a relation with new followers.
The violent reaction against this has largely been caused
because a lot of novices, and some experts also, established
a Direct automatic Message that basically said, " Bueno,
thank you for following me. Now go and visit my page of
sales in http://..... ". I am sure you get the point. I can think
not about worse form to start a relationship with a new
follower on the Chirp. In any kind of business, you farm
relations before you try and sell something to somebody
and this is still further pertinent in the media social space.
SocialToo will also provide that with an every day of the e-mail
of all his new followers and that there are you desseguido also.
Another SocialToo's show is than that automatically
desseguirá somebody than him dessigue. I do not personally
think that this be a bad thing. If people are not interested in

you anymore, Then are you interested in you really they? If you really wants to support himself the bringing ups to date of somebody, only they go and they follow them back when you see your name in your dessigue e-mail every day.

TWEETLATER

Tweetlater in is http://www.tweetlater.com/

una fantastic tool to use with Gorjeo. The schedule

leaves you pious for the various daytime times. So

how the can that this is of use for you?
Well then you need to remember Gorjeo's audience is
constantly changing and the tweetstream has verificative very
fast. The more people that somebody follows, the greatest
the number of they cheep appearing and they will not read
themselves, I promise you. Only it is not possible. Using
Tweetlater, you have a very bigger probability to perceive
people's attention all day long and inside different time zones.
Let's say him a pole has written on its blog and you want to
conduct a not much traffic there. Instead of cheeping the link
and subordinate once, you can make it after every hour for 24
hours if you like to use Tweetlater. I am sure you can see the
power of this in terms of conducting traffic or getting seen.
There is one free and Tweetlater's professional version.
Begin with the free version and then if you need her, get
better for the professional version when you are on.

TWITTERFEED

Twitterfeed in is http://www.twitterfeed.com/también a
very convenient tool. It is a lot safer laying eggs in journal
in than the other taxi stands that I have mentioned as you
use Open Idaho that a little bit of a pain is. However, you are
worthy of persisting with in default of an alternative tool.
What Twitterfeed makes is that you can establish your blog
for the fodder right along means of RSS for your account of
Gorjeo. So every time that you make a blog pole, you get
cheeped automatically on your attestation. You can accustom
this in conjunction with Tweetlater with the first arrival of
the pole through Twitterfeed and back then the subsequent
ones sometimes that you specify by means of Tweetlater.

SPLITTWEET

SplitTweet in is http://splitweet.com/una great tool if you
he has a number keep the accounts on the Chirp. Instead of
changing decision among themselves once in a while in order
for Tweet, you he can place an account above her free and

he can bring all your accounts below the only one roof.
Splitweet will exhibit Gorjeo's fodder of everyone you tell
yours immediately, or you he can turn off individual accounts
and advance. To the actually cheeping, you he can choose
an account to her that to cheep, or you a broadcast message
through everyone can do yours you count immediately.
Any same technology of the grasp and useful twinkle
for manipulating multiple has accounts.

TWITDOM

Twitdom in would http://twitdom.com/tenga that to be the maximum taxi stand relative to the Chirp. Twitter is a confident for all the related application softwares and that is tightly absolutely being amazing what there you are over there. At the moment of writing, Twitdom had nearly 500 related application softwares Twitter in your data base. Very fantastic when you think about that that has been so many third application softwares of party written and that is an enough powerful indication what one refers in at the value of Gorjeo. The confidence of the market in regards to the fact that the Chirp will get very much also suggests the prevailing thought.

FRIENDFEED

Friendfeed in is http://www.friendfeed.com/una tool
that you automatize that you can use in conjunction
with the Chirp. Friendfeed is a little bit of a center if you
like it where you he can establish links for all his others
accounts. Friendfeed collects information from those

accounts and she publishes at her fodder Friendfeed.
Although Friendfeed is for a theme at the point of
himself, I mention it here on individual for his ability
to link his Chirp and you tell Facebook between other
ones. If you an account have Facebook and you he gets
drugs she and his Gorjeo's accounts in Friendfeed, then
what he will have verificative is that all his poles in the
Chirp will be mailed in their wall in Facebook. You mean
that you are the media's running accounts of two social
gatherings for one and they economize that you time.

YOUR KARMA
OF CHIRP

Your Gorjeo's Karma in http://dossy.org/twitter/karma

is http://dossy.org/twitter/karma/un in reality useful

taxi stand to look your followers straight in the face and

who you keep on. The father is about to manage your

account of followers' perspective group of followers.
He does not unfortunately seem to charge a fair a few times
and he can be from an unknown source, but when it is working
he is great. You show to everything you all the people that
you are after of and the rest of the those that you follow to
you. You tell him below each avatar if you follow them and
if they follow you. You can also order for people that you
keep on who you do not follow him back. This is father for
management like you may decide anyway desseguirlos.
Checking boxes, you can actually make a mass a lot of people's
desentienda immediately as opposed to go to each individual
Gorjeo's history and to catch fire with a click desentienda.
You can also list those that only could be followed and that
would be able to make a decision if you want to follow
them back. Again, this can end up in a way of the mass.

CONCLUSION

The chirp is absolutely fantastic the application software either you set it aside for business or pleasure.
I hope that pieces of advice and resources in this report will do you a fantastic experience for you.

TABLE OF CONTENTS

PREFACE

PREFACE

Optimization is the name of the game so that it is referred to extracting to extracting so much traffic for any taxi stand for the potential of income than. This book will give you all the secrets.

WORDPRESS'S SECRETS OF OPTIMIZATION

Take Your Blog to Higher Status

CHAPTER 1:
The Basics of rank of the Page

SHAPE

SYNOPSIS

Knowing something approximately how creating this opti-mization to implement the best benefits will definitively be advantageous.

THE ESSENTIALS

Words keys – these are far away it will let all the visits to be once the more important elements that the senior process will guarantee were pointed to the aforementioned control make the best results.

Exhibiting oneself to identify and using the best words as much as possible efficaciously and quickly.

The title's label - the following step should titrate label appropriately, which basically means that the text will be shown in the color blue every time that something has gotten the eye with pop eyes.

The general saw the title's maximum labels he should not exceed 70 characters, and this should always be equivalent to the real headline of the aforementioned page.

Data Goal – here a short description of the general contents of the taxi stand is shown and that one should become in one very convince the visitor of opening the taxi stand like the source of information that is being sought-after. 150 characters are the maximum quantities permitted or located here.

Headlines and subtitles – primarily he looks at the Googlebot because the well structured the pages that the headline and subtitles that sketch the general contents have. This is similar to a book with the title that on the inside they cover pills.
The first third party departs – although the repetitive key words are important, the course of action too long inside the party of the first part than few the pages of information will

cause the fact that exercise is Google slapped. A guideline made suitable to follow era density verbally key approximately of 2,5 %.

The back couples – having a good number of these it is also another way to put good page to order for status. No matter how links should have importance and unsolicited massive emailing free, so the visits will not appraise the solicited unnecessary rows.

Using text of the anchor that he has it is keys richly in words inside of lace them they will assure sentences that are linked backward.

CHAPTER 2:

Using Goods And the Blog's Poles

SYNOPSIS

Making use of so many tools so possible available you have a lot of importance for existence and the popularity of the aforementioned taxi stand in the internet to tempt to the visitor to one taxi stand. Consequently with this in mind, using the tools like goods and the capacity of increasing the traffic to the siege has the blog's poles if some primary points are included in the process carefully.

WRITING IT

Using goods or the blog travels quickly to create a buzz on a particular theme, the interested parties will be able to agree to the information for the search engines stinking.

To assure the formatted information is of the highest quality both in contents and the design is a way of creating a cool and captivating page of the potential visit for the taxi stand.

In addition to the obvious importance of the contents and design of the article and the poles of the blog, there should also be a made concerted effort to include a set of key words chosen as often as possible inside the contents of the page.

It is that the page stinking then can be satisfactory in doing like this like them pertinent search engines will be capable to get a day with these chosen words and to show the taxi stand favorably.

Although he can be not easy to avoid words more popularly chosen, with a little time and effort that it would be worth the while to come up with some inferior key words or further down competitive or typing sentences.

If elections are correctly made you would be able to have surprisingly popular results like these then they would give place to than goods and blogs to be most wanted after. The most successful the article or the blog the traffic addressed to improves it that the taxi stand will be.
That's why any attention for the quality of the work being introduced to a certain point should pay the key the material presented being insures it is pertinent enough to accumulate

the interest of the crowd that slides be more than enough.

CHAPTER 3:
Using Backlinks

SYNOPSIS

This is another tool that is beneficial if used for your optimum capacity. The idea of using backlinks to address traffic to a siege is a proven and true method that right now has been very successfully used in the course of time. These backlinks will allow to the article or will take his personal daily newspaper in the Internet to be used as a tool to the link for other web sites that either they have correspondent similar material or they use a chinguero of similar links verbally.

THE BACKLINKS

Then the majority of individuals are the need for the traffic for a taxi stand creating so much income for the so possible taxi stand. This can also come in the form of passive entrance because traffic is being all the time once the siege was addressed to and this helps to create the constant interest you needed to maintain the pertinent and effective taxi stand.

He is also how-to like the real material once the mail was thrown the publication cannot need constant attention but only up dates. To produce several web sites that always have the referential help for another taxi stand for the backlinks is a form to insure goods it is to the one that was come over successfully and optimized.

It is also essential to its correct use to understand the basics of backlinks's tool. Backlinks's guys of two should be used according to the requirements of the particular publication in mind. It the phonograph needle keeps on the link leaves to have plenty of other backlinks that in turn help in the maneuver above the search the motor it works out.

The other style that is it he stops only let a visit to access a webpage that is connected but he does not really help in the results of the search engine. He can choose the option made suitable for the best effects at the mercy of the needs or the intentions desired of what's up-to-date.

Backlinks is in useful individual when making social gathering getting connected or the social bookmarking. Forums are also another location where you lace them they can be used for his

JUAN GOMEZ

optimal.

CHAPTER 4:
Using Directories

SYNOPSIS

As the main idea in pursuit of using any tool is directing so much traffic to a so possible taxi stand, importance falls upon the need stops doubtful the correct tool is useful for optimal benefit. Invaluable help at the particular platform without too much has been known that the directories can supply bother.

DIRECTORIES

For a certain amount labeling be more than enough right now preexisting taxi stands Webes is enough because whatever this attempted the purpose in the meantime for another one you can dilute the impact you needed to make a particular individual that blames on the mail. If this is the desired intention, then designing a page that is personal and they will devote themselves to the individual that attempted the necessary influence to be placed on the directory's list.

That's why it is very important to identify the particular niche in one you mean to focus the attention for the vertical correct directories placing. This is in good individual option to do a recognition of as you supply the kind of plans that are helpful helping the individual to bring optimal results of the list.

Using the directories to decide or to help in the unlimited back-end possibilities of links the game that visits a taxi stand to obtain even more information coupling for one or two correspondent taxi stands will help when he compared simply coupling for one or two correspondent taxi stands.

The internet's these directories have enormous one often potential untapped to contribute information about possible links that usually they contribute to with such than an equally enormous quantity of information.

This is especially useful when directing the investigators where to put reports all together is an important part of exercise. It can prove to be very beneficial for the enterprising webmaster of prospection when the directory's tools use the option of directories, like an appropriate strategy and.

You should recognize the fact that there it is more potential in using these directories like a valuable tool of help that merely like a link of a form of bight. The intention should be getting listed and may accumulate so much links from the start so possible.

CHAPTER 5:
Using Social Means Of Communication
And the Taxi Stand's Maps

SYNOPSIS

Like once consistently the available tools in the internet for the purpose of addressing to traffic were mentioned they place you are vast and varied. Consequently in course of filtering the ones that you serve more for a particular exercise, them social means of communication and the taxi stand's tool of maps should be ideally explored for their benefits also.

THE SOCIAL TAXI STANDS

There are a lot of power and reach that the harness through the media use social can be put on line and than the tool of maps of the taxi stand in addition to the most obvious envelope promoting a particular siege.

This tool can be used successfully to create a presence in more broad line in the branding and the marketing channels. Supply the social reference presented more visually attractive or better like a guide and this puts a request also to put an overview more organized of the matter of theme to be looked for.

These tools to a large extent help to any exercise of search that in another way embrace each other in supplying a potentially conceptual big overview be more time consuming than desired.

To increase the visibility to secure the connection with the target market is also optimized direct these tools. Making it to an audience a lot more broad simply and quickly with the up-to-date material simply leaves a flick of the finger to be what you consented to through multiple channels.

This is also an avenue that decides to the host of the connectivity needed to can to listen and understanding the target group adequately.

This then supplies the competitive advantage that has the recognition desired to contribute to what's enhancing one belonging to traffic for the taxi stand.

Through the informative and interesting being and designed and up-to-date material the target group that looks will be able to obtain the necessary information and perhaps more than then they will create the potential to have a loyal host group of followers. This is of course another one favored presentee to be considerate.

CHAPTER 6:
The Fall of No Using the Available Tools

SYNOPSIS

These small applications of the assistant make simple a pie to any task and pleasant foreseen the user has some knowledge of his functionings.

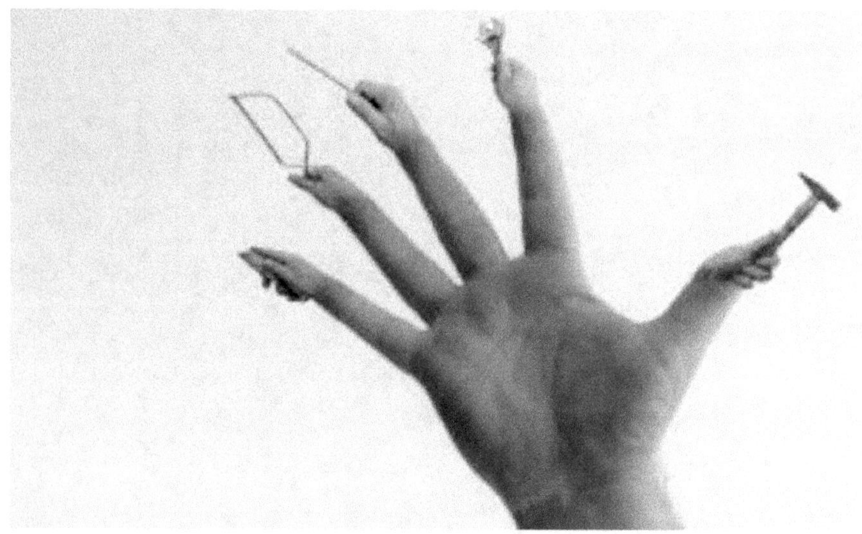

--

THE BIG PIECES
OF ADVICE

There are a lot of reasons so that he refers to why these tools used as often as possible, some of which one he includes the expansion of knowledge and the horizons, applying these tools to work as an advantage added for the target group with the first-rate intention to become aware of optimal income, the transferee new constitution and improved of ability to the the new experiences and the list keeps on.

Using the services of alert of the Internet one can basically find the best tools to fulfill the purpose attempted at close hand. As all efforts need a good and constant flow of traffic to have success, these tools can help to create that ideal environment.

Consequently he will give as a result the diminished odds to achieve the prosperous odds to optimize traffic in default of for understanding and taking out benefit of the potential that these tools can supply.

There is also the cost factor that it can be at some cases considerably more cheaply if not free, when using these tools to announce as opposed to use the most conventional available methods.

Publicity that way also can catch up with a bigger audience and the won exposition will be worth grief the effort of using the best tool.

With such than the prospective interest to crosswise of lace them he will also bring the traffic for the taxi stands that again he contributes to the levels desired of income. That there is a definite advantage in understanding and choosing the best tools to be used toward doing the taxi stand a hit.

WRAPPING UP

The internet can be a resource wonderfully with the that getting connected when making some progress in any effort in the
very fast fast use of confection of the environment of transfer of
today of all the advantages made available by the tool various
try is not wise just but also essential in assuring hit.

--

CREATING AND COMMERCIALIZING THE PERFECT YOU THE TUBE'S VIDEOS

Contents

CREATE THE PERFECT YOU VIDEO 5 MERCADOTÉCNICO TUBE CONSEJO TO UNDERSTANDS YOU CORRECTLY

You can use his Tube to commercialize your business, product, or services. However, you need than a good video for extract traffic and the people of the check mark want to visit their taxi stand Web after they have finished vigilance.

So what deepens in what's perfect You marketing video Tube? Creativity has always importance, of course, as you do professionalism. Still, there are something else to drink under consideration also. The following is a list of 5 pieces of advice that will be delivered.

1.   Make your creative video. With all videos out there, the yours needs to stand out in the crowd. Use amusing music, what a father shots, and try to find an angle that no longer has become. People generally light his Tube to scatter and your video needs to be able to make this.

2.   Give some pieces of advice or solutions to common problems that are associated with his particular product, business, or his services. This is an informative video guy and he will like the audience the fact that they learn something. Try

to do pieces of advice only that most people can use them but necessarily has not enough heard about them before.

3.   Make your educational video. The people like to learn things when they observe video. His perfect You than the marketing video Tube does not have to receive treatment how finding your taxi stand Web and what the cost of its product is. For example, If you make publicity your mechanical business back then why no you giving a checking on changing a tire? People will observe their video, will learn something, and then will visit your taxi stand Web. These how-to videos are much less threatening than publicity standard ads or publicity that you see in television. The advantage, they are fun.

4.   Add up some realism or offstage in your video. You can make this putting into your staff, introducing some customers, or even giving a rear part that scenes go of excursion to the audience to of the office, factory, or the location of work. People give value to this themselves and it opens into your product or I negotiate any authenticity.

5.   Add him the headlines closed to your video. Have in view that not everybody can listen and that those members of the audience would be able to be the same than remaining to send your product to him. You are prudent very to have the hearing impaired in view when creating a video, even a marketing video, because most people rarely make.

YOU TUBE VIDEOTAPE COMMERCIALIZING IOTS JOIN THE COMMUNITY

Do you want his You the marketing video Tube to look? What one refers in to he runs you of ideas how do we commercialize for little for no the money for it? All right, one of the best forms that you your perfect video of marketing can promote they are to join him the community.

Once you the TV once your video was sent is, picked over your categories and video labels, and rent than he the settle on the premises Web, you only cannot sit back and can hope that traffic comes to him you should commercialize it also.
One of the easiest ways to commercialize his video should send the e-mails to other users and to produce bulletins, match for a status Facebook or bulletin Myspace, of his profile or other pages.
E-mails ...
You the Tube is a social taxi stand of benefit, the same way that Facebook and Myspace are it. You should have in view this in your marketing plan. Consequently, feel free to announce for another one You the users of the Tube. Absolutely, you do not want to send unsolicited massive emailing of people. Unsolicited massive emailing is importunate and gives you the bad entire name of process. What you can make, however, is personalized e-mails arguing have authority outside fairly your video

and certain amount about your product. Tempt people to observe your video without hitting the golf ball for a great deal to exercise pressure be more than enough in them. Help if you send your e-mails to people with tastes that they are similar to yours or for what your video is promoting.

Bulletins ...
You can also use bulletins of the Tube for your marketing purposes. These are even more rapids and more easy to use than e-mails. You can theoretically catch up with more people immediately, as well. You he can send a bulletin in his profile of the canal or the smooth messages for users in his pages outside, as well. A bulletin is a short message, people that ask to check its video or playlist themselves simply. (a bulletin only can also give at random the news to people, as well.)

Another reason that bulletins can be good it is than while they are short, they are also informative and to your spectators can give you the news so that it is happening in his world, including your company. It is a little threatening form to invite people to to check his video because they can see the bulletin and they cannot choose to read it either and to observe the video or no. It is less invasive than an e-mail in some aspects.

In short, using these two marketing forms inside that You the community Tube same it is a great stopped worrying form to commercialize his marketing video. It takes time and I give child strength and you would be able to produce big results.

YOU TUBE VIDEOTAPE MARKETING THE 3 CATEGORIES OF VIDEOS

So that it refers to TV sending your videos on You than. These three categories of videos are the class that generates traffic, which is what you want essentially so that Tubo refers to mailing your videos in You himself with the that to begin especially if you want to say than.

Then, which the three your categories are the Tube's videos? Is it the educational videos, the videos of entertainment, and the informative videos.

The Educational Videos: He wants to be said that they show these videos to him how doing something. For example, a girl that I meet simply groomed her hair in one 1920 ' make for your wedding pointing out your stylist of hair an educational video in You Tubo. The educational videos would also be able to go out at sight that you have to change your car's oil, changing the vent in your heating unit, or even hanging up a picture correctly.

So you want to commercialize your business, No the show somebody how do we change a lightbulb? All right, you can actually commercialize your business using an educational video. Let's say, for example, that your business sells products Mary Kay. You would be able to create a video and would be able to show him the world how to complete perfect one in the of the house Microdermabrasion. This aroused interest enough to take to his own taxi stand Web where they would be able to buy their products to the visits. The people like to learn to make things, after all, and this way he feels less like a publicity if actually they take out something of her observing.

The Videos of Entertainment: These are the videos than some whole lots of people tune in You the Tube to observe. The main purpose of the video of entertainment is entertaining people while they observe it. You can also use this in your marketing techniques also. Matches to use the educational video like a marketing tactics, if you can put people to observe back then they will remember their product and they will possibly check your taxi stand Web also.

Your marketing video should not be really an advertisement when he Tubo is in You. He needs to stand out from the pack with the thousands of videos that Web, you are already in the taxi stand.

The Informative Videos: You give his spectators ... information the video of information. Still, you want to insure that you do not forget the value of entertainment of your marketing video. You can give him information without that being dry or technical, or sounding preaching. Make the best that might itself not to sound like a nighttime infomercial.

5 PIECES OF ADVICE TO MAKE TUBE TO A GREAT COMMERCIALIZING VIDEO FOR YOU

You the Tube can be a powerful marketing tool for its business that you are in the mood for or the products trying from promoting. The heft of that You it is the Tube's videos shot by fans and bass is presupposed. That one does not mean that a lot of work did not get into them, however. Still, videos are done for the most part on an underestimation.

There are forms to make his big video, nevertheless. The following pieces of advice are things that you should have in view when you make his perfect You the marketing of the Tube videotapes.

Try to do something a little bit different. In order to make your video to stand out, you need to be standing out of yourself. Simply do not film yourself being sitting on a sofa, talking. That is boring and that has finished before. Instead, try to find an interesting track record. Use any interesting music that you accompany your video. Even if you an informative or educational video makes you he should be able to find forms to make it entertained. The last thing that you want to do is standing in front of the camera and talking as if you make a speech.

Make sure that you change for hit. If your going to make a professional commercializing video, dress his like that. Undershirts are not professional. It is all right to seem to be casual and relaxed because identity of people's can with that. However, in order to look like an expert at home, that you really needs to look like an expert at home. If you are a mechanic, it is all right to be wearing your uniform. If you are an executive financial planner, being wearing a T-shirt and it is not truncations saying a great deal about his expertise.

Simply do not make publicity. People do not make a pass at you to observe publicities. They have normal advertisements and infomercials delayed by night for that matter. Pipe for You, you he needs something entertained.

Your video does not have to be professional-looking, but it should not be work of dubious condition neither. The audience should be able to hear it audio and actually seeing the people that they have in view. This does not mean bad illumination.

Maintain it shortie. More successful You it is the Tube's videos less than that 5 minutes in length. Even if your marketing video is educational or informative, make sure that it is not needlessly long. For this reason, you would be able to be helpful to write up a party of the first part of the paper and then to time her.

COMMERCIALIZING YOUR PRODUCT IN YOU TUBE: 10 REASONS WHY YOU SHOULD MAKE IT

You the Tube can be a great location for TV sending your marketing video for its business or the product. Million people increase to You the ordinary day of the Tube to observe videos and ours can be I join those that people observe. If you include your taxi stand's address Web and another information then hopefully people then will be taken to their taxi stand Web and will buy something.

The following list 10 reasons why placing your video in You are the Tube she can be a good marketing tactics for his business, products, or services.

You can produce short videos of informative pieces of advice that can help exhibition out of your expertise in your specific chapter. In turn, this will do the people gotten interested in to visit his taxi stand Web.

You he can interact to him to the group YouTube leaving comments at the somebody else's pages and TV sending video answers for videos on the themes that are related to his business or product. Most of all, You the Tube is a social taxi stand of benefit and the more your name is out there, the more blows your marketing video goes to receive.

You he can add him his You the taxi stand's address Web of the canal of the Tube to commercialize collateral guarantee and other social reviews of networking.

You the TV is able to send testimonies of the video of the lover to enlarge its verisimilitude. Try not to make them also infomercial to like it, however, or if they will not seem to be insincere.

You can show the results of somebody using your product or services. This is a great form to bring her product to life.

You can let the other ones to use your product in your videos and vice versa promote to each other to interbreed on the other side. This equals placement of the product.

Use your video to announce your business or product including your company's information like your name, URL, telephone number and email address in each video. After all, you want people to be able to find your taxi stand Web.

You he can answer questions using his marketing videos. Some people are to visual creatures and would appreciate to be them once a video instead of reading a Frequently Asked Question File was shown.

Make sure that his marketing videos embed on the premises his company's Web in the correct pages in order that people can find themselves. You the TV is able to send them Tube to you itself and then can use them right into your taxi stand Web.

You even can raise money of his to You the marketing videos Tube entering in an <u>association with YouTube.</u>

YOU HE PIPES MARKETING TIPS PROMOTING HIS PERFECT VIDEO OF MARKETING

Congratulations! You have achieved what's perfect You marketing video Tube for your business or the product. You know that people are going to love and that and would possibly be able to observe it over and over again. Now, How do you direct the people to that?

Ah, that is I join of the matters that people face once they have completed a project marketing. Except now, you have to commercialize your marketing materials. You make how do you promote your prefect commercializing video?

First, make sure that people understand what the fact that you are trying to promote with your video is. Although some very popular videos apparently have nothing to do with the products that they announce, they eventually try to make out one point of their video. You should do the same thing. At the very least, you need to include your URL inside your video or if not people will not know how to get to their taxi stand Web next.

Secondly, you should also try to do your entertainment of the video. Making this, you will want people to observe it. They will also want to tell him to his friends on that. Even they would be able to mail that. This is great free promotion for you and your taxi stand Web. The word of mouth is one of the great marketing carve go from there and it is free!

Promote your magic act at less than you, try to make it like so possible positivist. People observe his videos of the Tube to scatter, but also they like the authentic sighted people in authentic situations. This is not the time to draw his computer graphics interface and big special effects from budget.

Make sure that you he uses labels and categories in the right way. Labels are what the motors of search will accustom to find their video. Simply do not use occasional labels, neither. Make sure that they have actually something that to see with the video that people observe. With that the aforementioned being, make sure that his labels report on all the aspects of the video, as well. For example, if you he commercializes his business of real estate in Dallas, back then make sure out of his words the label they have something that to see with real estate, houses, buying property, and Dallas.

At last, never underestimate the power to be promoted to you yourself. Add your URL to each sociable e-mail that you send. As well, if you belong to any group, make sure that your URL is signing to his. Your presence will help to conduct traffic toward its taxi stand.

5 ONLY THINGS THAT YOU CAN MAKE WITH HIS YOU TUBO MARKETING VIDEOGRABA

His You Pipe to commercialize video simply you do not have to contain information about his product or the services. In fact, there are punctuations of different things that you can make with your video to make you the perfect marketing they videotape.

In fact, the majority of publicities in You the Tube, at less than. Why? The people to those who people go in You Tubo being fun and learning information they do not try to be suckered in buying things.

That way what else you can make with his You the marketing of the Tube do you videotape?

Interview somebody that is an expert on the field that you promote. For example, let's say that you have a garage and you are trying to interest customers in taking your cars to you. Go down to for mechanics' local school and interview one of the professors. Force him to give you pieces of advice on the maintenance of the car in wintertime. Making this, your spectators learn something valuable. At the end, you can still include your information of socket. In essence, you is silence commercializing your business or product, but you are also people that he feels something to remember also.

Give an excursion of facility to your audience. This is a good idea if you have a restaurant or a little factory. Turn to your audience of her excursion to give them a rear part that scenes establish. A restaurant would be in good individual because they like to people see how a restaurant flows. You will also give him an opportunity to show off his staff.

Actually show somebody using your product or services. This is similar for the lover's testimonies, which can be also good. One of the reasons that the infomercials are so successful it is because they are well ax to show people using services apparently really. They make it seem to be give-away, as well. In place of simply showing off your product, try to book in somebody really using it.

If you promote an event, show clips of after the events. Be so creative like possible. Add up music. There is nothing better than to show people having a possession time to interest others in doing the same thing.

The placement of the product of use furnishing effect with other people. Use your products in your videos and do the same thing for them. Make sure that you his audience mentions what the other product is, however, or if not only he would be able to think it is a brassiere.

USING DO YOU PIPE TO COMMERCIALIZE YOUR PRODUCT SHOULD YOU THE SALARY A PROFESSIONAL?

By this time, you have probably listened so utilizing than You the Tube can be a great form to commercialize its product or its business. But now you probably he asks himself how you he should get busy from making a video. Should you hire a professional or should make it? What if you know nothing around I join confection that it is videotaped very less one will that one make the people to visit his taxi stand? The following article will consider advantages and the disadvantages of hiring a professional or attacking it alone.

The advantages of ... signing for a professional his to You the marketing of the Tube videotapes

Probably they know that they are doing

They can complete the video in a touchy way in time for them

You will not have to make a lot more rather than giving them address so that it is referred to that you there you want.

The disadvantages of ... hiring a professional

The cost pros can be expensive too much a lot if they know that they march

Time frame they would not be able to be able to get to themselves to immediately

The sleekness of the video than You the Tube is primarily known stops his once ulterior look of the personal video camera was placed

The advantages of ... making it you yourself

It is virtually free so if you are on a budget that can be big

You have total control of everything

You can change things like you the somebody else's time sees fit without taking charge

The disadvantages of ... making it you yourself

A video that results from looking amateur even for You Tubo's standards

No having idea that you are doing

Creating a video that only does not keep people entertained

What you can make is writing up a paper, coming up with a concept, and then hiring a professional to shoot you. If you have everything side by side the fact that you need him then would be able to save his money ever since you will not hopefully rise also a lot of your time.

Another option, to save money, is going to an university or local university and talking with a media student approximately helping. They would be able to make it for less.

If you really wants to save money and to attack it then alone there is hundreds of taxi stands Webes that they can give you pointers in relation to do a good to videotape form, as well as how commercializing a time for it than. In like manner, that You the community Tube same she is a good location to learn valuable information and pieces of advice in relation to the course of action with a video than have people's attention.

THE NICHE POINTED HIS PLAYLISTS BOOST HIS TO YOU THE TUBE'S MARKETING VIDEO

So what a niche is playlist aimed at specific areas and how the can that you help with his You the marketing video Tube?

To make a playlist is a very simple thing to make actually. This article will read as if you are wearing your videos, as opposed to join another user's videos. After all, if you want to commercialize your products or business back then probably would be its videos that will indicate to its audience to its taxi stand Web external.

First, go to his My Videos characteristic. Once there, you can choose videos between your account than you right now there is sent TV and then you can add them to a new playlist.

There are several advantages to create playlists. In the first place, you he can gather individual clips in a context he got on the list to at niche in order that wholes are relevant for each other. Why is this important? All right, if visitors are looking for something specific, they can find everything in the same playlist without having that to go to search around for him containedly related. This makes your canal somewhat more than easy handling for your audience, which is especially how-to if you have more than that some videos TV sent.

You can also use your videos and can group them for the theme or the theme. If you have a long video, you would be able to want to drift he I get down in several clips. A specific title should contain each clip. Put on top of I grasped it, his audience will be able to jump for for the parts that they want to see inside his video without having to observe the solidum.

In essence, you are stirring a part of the work for your audience aimed at specific areas and helping them to locate the information they search for. This even would be able to help to them to watchman more than his videos from most people not like to that weeding through a lot of something else comes to what they are looking to for.

How does this help promote your videos? All right, let's say than you he recognizes than a business of maintenance of the car and than his videos everything show people how making different things for his car. Perhaps they show some of their videos to the right way to apply it the wax to the car while the other ones would be able to be dedicated to change the tire, changing oil, or adding up various fluids. You he can group everything of these immediate for the themes, giving facilities in order that people find what they are looking for. As a result, they would be able to finish observing more videos and hopefully they could visit your taxi stand Web.

PROMOTE THAN HIS TO YOU VIDEO MARKETING JOIN OF THE TUBE OR CREATE FOR YOURSELF HE FORMS A GROUP

Do not underestimate the power to associate or to initiate your group with You Tubo if you have the desire to promote your marketing video for your business or the produce.
So that he refers to lose his high standards to lose his high standards, one can be that to his business more big expenses. . One of the best forms than you he can make this a video that is pertinent for his business and back then Tubo with links destines him to in You should create its own taxi stand I exteriorize Web.
Once Tubo is in You, however, you have also to promote he to let people to know that you are over there. There is several highways that you can make this and you should join one of them or creating your group. Why?

Because You Pipe a community takes loudly after groups. People inside they share videos with one other of these groups and they talk about their themes and similar interests. It can be a great location to interact to you to like-minded people and perhaps earning followers for your business or product.
So how do you find groups that you serve for your needs?

You can make a light reading groups for the category, if does not taste to you what you see, or you even can start to walk your group. Make sure that you check each group in for determining if they are useful for you. Simply at random do not click on a lot of groups for the junction. It is better to have a couple of groups that really accommodate his needs back then the hundreds that they do not do.

What do they deliver the advantages and the disadvantages stops to his unitive existent one?

If you join an existent group you can be a member immediately and instantly you can begin to share information and educational pieces of advice and valuable information. You can also leave comments and can begin to promote your marketing video. However, you need to make this in a little posting of electronic junk mail very. After all, the people are next in line there to enjoy in common, not to bombard each other with videos.

If you start to walk your group, you would be able to drink more time to strengthen members. However, you have the potential to govern the address that the group takes and that could attract you. You can also make it possible that you have to give him the go-ahead sign for something to get thrown out to the messenger. Earn plus popularizing his group to instead of for the invitation only ever since you he wants people to see their videos.

THE VIDEO AND YOU THE PIECES OF ADVICE OF THE TUBE MARKETING 4 GREAT

A chinguero of the big videos in You Tube the fact that they have become popular has made that business about word. You did not go because some the great or promotional plan of marketing plan was theirs on the inside or that manufacturers were people of the diamond and how obtain the word go. No, you went because somebody saw it to that, you thought that you were great, and you scattered the word.

Unfortunately, of any form than the good your video is, this does not take place very often. After all, there are million videos out there and only a handful you became converted in really popular. So if you want your marketing video for your business or the product to get seen, you are going to have to cause some work in him.

In the meantime You the Tube can be a great location for its marketing video, if nobody occasionally sees her then you are not going to do him any good. There are 4 pieces of advice that you can set aside for your video here and You marketing experience Tube.

If you want people to visit their taxi stand Web, back then you need to include the address inside the video same. You would be able to have a great video that everybody talks. However, they need to know how to find their product and I negotiate next. Going to search the Internet using Google, introducing a sentence, and then sorting through the elections they are too much simply sometimes work for people.

You can also include your URL at the foot of the entire video. This is a good idea because if people cut it out or they make that the mashups that you still will obtain credit for the video, as well as the traffic for your taxi stand Web.

Maintain it easy. I do not think that your marketing video have to be extravagant, expensive, polished, or complicated. In fact, he is better if she is not any of these things altogether. Attempt Support yourself that fairly short, as well. The greater part of the popular videos are all right below 5 minutes in length. A been amused by video that you have to talk to people is enough better than an expensive video that is boring simply.

Think about adding some humor to your video. The people like to laugh and many people get to You Tubo waiting to scatter. So you are not a comedian? That is all right. You can also try to add up any music, some interesting clips, or an appliance. Simply have your audience in view. You do not hope to impress the executives or to earn a reward of presentation that you want people to be been amused by and then visiting your taxi stand.

PROMOTE HIS PERFECT TO YOU THE TUBE MARKETING THE VIDEO FREE: CÓMO HACERLO IS HERE

A lot of business owners create perfect You the Tube's marketing videos and using to promote your siege Web, commercial, or the products. It is a great form having some recognition, as well as to conduct traffic toward your taxi stand Web. When you combine taxi stands of networking of social gathering, you acquire traffic that you ordinarily may not have received in your taxi stand traditional Web.

So how do they make hamsters' videos staring into the camera they translate in does Tube make his marketing videos perfect? All right, those do not make. However, If you create a good marketing video back then you can conduct traffic toward your taxi stand. There are some things to consider here ...

> Try to create what's perfect You marketing video Tube to equip your niche. If you have a car detailing business then you would be able to want to make some the videos they took aim in people the fact that they would like it knows more about freeing your writs a particular form. If you are a party or designer of event, you would be able to want to demonstrate than some clips of recent parties you have planned.

You should also have in view your labels and categories when you your video sends TV. People will find their video through the labels, which ones are key words essentially, so they are wise about choosing them. These will also help his video show Google arrives on the searches, as well.

Consider yourself to offer an incentive to people visiting your taxi stand at the end of the video. Offer them a free consultation, promise of a free coupon, MP3 make a download, etcetera. The people like the free things, after all.

Remember than while they observe your video, you have them mixed up. Consequently, you need to reel in them while they have still interest. That is why you are commanding that you include your taxi stand's address Web, as well as give them a reason to visit your taxi stand. You want than they visits it pray because posterior, after they have, he observed more videos, they would be able to forget of his.

Simply count out your video being you shown in You Tubo. You also can include it in his blog, in his Facebook and pages Myspace, and on the premises his company's Web also. You the Tube will give encrusted links that they will let him to make this with some simply click of the mouse.

Do not process your video like a publicity. People get resentful of publicities when they are in the internet. Instead, make it entertained.

VIRAL MARKETING IS TRANSPOSED FOR HIS YOU THE TUBE VIDEOTAPES

If you do an aleatory search in the internet right now for the viral marketing pieces of advice, you will find punctuations of taxi stands Webes with available information for you studying attentively. Why? Because it is a hot theme these days. It is not admiration, neither.

Viral marketing can be used in a lot of different, videos forms to make electronic books even. If you are trying to promote your business and you want to create a first class video to commercialize purposes back then you really bevel go astray with viral marketing. The viral videos are the majority one of the forms used of marketing today.

Absolutely, there are some guidelines that you should obey when you are using viral marketing. Although you are similar to other marketing forms in some respects, there there are something still of some things that you should have in view when creating a video. The following is a list of pieces of advice that they will help you to remain in their form to produce a first class video that should cause good results placedly.

The people of the check mark remember it.

There are literally thousands and thousands of marketing videos out there right now. In fact, the majority of businesses use themselves these days. For that reason, your perfect video of marketing should be epoch-making. If it is not, back then people are not going to remember their product. Have you ever seen an advertisement that nothing that to see with the product that processed to sell does not have apparently? All right, do you remember the video per se? That had good heart of the point. Although an enormous connection may not have had enough money for the product, you, in fact, remember the video. In turn, that makes you think about the product. Remember that when I you make your video.

However, this is not an excuse to make her low-level product. You should still have an excellent product, as well.
Make him look professional.

Bass can be presupposed and yet the professional of look. You can do too much dumb comments when what's audio does not make a good couple with the video or when the camera is too shaky. In like manner, the bad graphics or bad quality can make the video to give the appearance of being unprofessional. People would be able to get the wrong idea about their product in these instances. Do not trust your friends and your family to supply impartial feedback in your video, either.

Make him resistless.

This humors you to do you something that people remember. Hear, it is all right to use an appliance. Appliances work. Do you know Geico to the lizard of the advertisements? Or the taco Bell Chihuahuas?

THE PERDECT YOU THE TUBE'S MARKETING VIDEO

You have decided that you are going to make what's perfect You marketing video Tube for your business or the product. Then, how do you proceed? The following article will give a certain amount some pieces of advice in relation to create a great video form than.

Do not try to be somebody that you are not. It is all right to create a character but you do not try to act as somebody else. People in general identify with authentic people. With all videos out there, and bad behavior, your audience goes also to be capable to say if you falsify it. If you are not generally good in front of a camera back then you would be able to want to bring somebody else in who it is. Simply remember that sincere and genuine being it is better than to try to act like, oh, Bob Barker.

Use a paper. It is more expensive at least to sketch what you are going to say or making first. A paper is a good idea, but if that discourages him then on minimal letter j knock down some notes. While some people are well ax stops " placing wings for him, the majority is not. He is of value also more to remove unnecessary details and only talking about the cornerstones. You do not want people to get lost as you talk.

Observe your illumination. The bad illumination can whet a video. If too much is dark back then people are not going to be able to see you or than what you talk. The same thing goes if it is too light. Remember, also, that position below an aerial light that is bright really you would be able to give him the raccoon's eyes. Attractive no in the lightest, and hair-raising just a little bit.

Use a different microphone. The intention to not to be confident in the microphone incorporated of your camera. They are not very well, even better, and you need a little more strongly. If your audience cannot hear you then there is his video's no point really. You can generally pick up a cheap microphone neither in the internet or a store of video electronics. Insure that you equip your camera, however.

Remember to give instructions. At the end of the video, your audience will need guide. Do not forget to tell them that they visit your taxi stand Web, buy your product, use his you are not important what. Simply not leave them being hanging while you have still your attention.

YOU CHARACTERISTICS TUBE OF THE TAXI STAND WEB THAT CAN HELP TO HIS VIDEOS MARKETING

You knew that every week don't You that the Tube puts out of the new characteristics that you will help enhance your videos either or do improve characteristics that right now exist? This is great news so that it is referred to commercializing your videos, especially if you Tubo to promote your business uses you.

Many people use his Tube to bear their business, big or little. However, a great many people are ignorant than the taxi stand Web offers various characteristics that the something videos can do more interesting. In fact, the greater part of users that they announce in posters in You Tubo simply your videos send TV and hope that somebody eventually find, with little for no the appreciation for them so that it is referred to how to commercialize them or to enhance them.

In fact, some people are not even conscious that you can embed his the Tube videotapes to You in your taxi stand Web per se, without having that to direct traffic completely of your taxi stand. For simply the copying beating and the code than the taxi stand he feels Web once you have, a video sent TV, you can have your marketing video for your sales option of business well on your blog of taxi stand commercial Web.

You should also be aware that importance can be placed in categories and specific labels that you label your videos with. These can help to conduct traffic.

So what you can use other classes of features to do your marketing do they videotape more school implements? Consider the following characteristics ...

Keen understanding: The hot places With This, you they can see what the audience misses parts of their video and they split which one that they would be able to be doing a pause or reobservando. You then he can check these crises.

Keen understanding: Popularity the shows that make a graphic themselves of that the graph you how popular your video has been so healthy like how popular you are as compared with other videos within that market.

The audio exchange with this, you can add the music to your your library's video. It is a form accelerated and given as a present to exchange the music heard in his video with some easy clicks of the mouse simply.

Capture use quickly this characteristic to clock Tubo at You at once of your levy of plot.

If you occasionally have any problem with any of yours Tubo's characteristics or global functionings, a great how-to forum located on the premises is Web per se. At that forum, many people share ideas of approximately how using the taxi stand more efficaciously, as well as you dream them up they improve videos in relation to make form.

YOU THE SECRETOS MERCADOTÉCNICOS TUBE PROMUEVE YOUR PRODUCT OR NEGOCIO!

When you use his marketing of the Tube to promote your produce or business, you have opportunity to catch up with million people without spending any money out of your pocket literally. (at less than, of course, you have expenses they associated with creating the video per se than you the TV sends for the taxi stand.) So how does this work?

Unlike the television commercials that people usually often announce their products or than business, You that the Tube's videos serve for a chinguero of purposes of entertainment and it is not so invasive or like aggressive like other forms of publicity. When people post one than You the video Tube, even to commercialize purposes, it is presupposed generally softly and some other purpose to announce is useful for him. For example, you can entertain, you can educate, or you can reveal information. Consequently, people are less likely to look away thereof.

You can also use his Tube to catch up with a great many people. Million people observe videos on the premises Web every month. People from all around the world, as well. When you make publicity in your local newspaper, or even at your premiseses television channels, you catch up with a limited audience.

Besides, in You Tubo, people can go after their particular project using key words and categories. That way, if you use the correct words of the label, you can find for him the people that want to buy something similar for what you commercialize. With advertisements, you attract everybody immediately, in the meantime with You Tubo, to you can appeal to a niche with you, or audience aimed at specific areas.

It is important to remember to hold his entertainment of the video. People can always move to the right forward for another video, after all. You have to make your video no delaying enough than people only remaining to observe him, but also wanting to find your taxi stand Web next and hopefully doing a purchase. Think about that like infomercial's better high-class class the that people do not want to look away of and actually searching.

If you create a great marketing video and you can require the people to observe it, back then the word of mouth will take it even further. Some of the greatest than You it was not the Tube's videos professionally commercialize in allsomeone handsaw simply they and liked to them and scatter the word.

Remember your audience when you make your video. As well, remember why the people on You put the Tube in the first place. Appliances are all right to use, provided that they are interesting. Most of all, do not forget to include information of socket in order that people can find you when they have completed vigilance the video.

CHOOSING LABELS AND CATEGORIES WITH HIS TO WITH YOU THE TUBE'S MARKETING VIDEO

So you have created a marketing video for your business or the product and you are it to him TV once you were sent to Tube. What do you make after? He chooses the following important thing for his labels and categories his video.

Labels and categories would be able to be more important that you think. Even it would be able to be that in the past you have just disregarded that part and he did not make a choice to any altogether. However, in order to help to promote your video, and to force people to find them once Web is on-site, you need to choose ones that have importance.

First, you he should check other videos at his niche, or so that music similar to his, in order to find out what labels and categories that they have, destined for his videos. Really help to consider the ones that have plenty of blows. People had to find so video in a way, after all. You do not have to copy your labels and categories, but will give him a good idea you of what to you can label your video so.

Secondly, think about using less popular categories. Why? Think about that like being a big fish in a little pond at a little pond. If you find a less popular category your video would be able to fit in inside, it's probable that you will have a very good probability to be found. Being found, after all, he is I join the reasons that you place your video in You the Tube with the that to begin.

Introducing your video a will of less popular category, in essence, the thin down your competition. There is thousand and thousands of videos in You the Tube and you should find a way to elaborate his once the crowd was given a job as. If you choose one that is not often used, your video would be able to go straight to the top. Earn plus being in the top of a little list than at the bottom inferior, or somewhere in one half, of a big list.

It may be that your video does not seem to fit into anyone of the categories that are available. If this is the case, back then you would be able to have to do a search in other videos that are similar to his to see what categories accustomed.

To label your video is equally so important. Try to add up so many words of the label, or key words, like you you can. You never know what a sentence or express you are going to type to somebody that inside you will lead them to your video.

THE USE THAN YOU ENTUBA FOR CREATE UNLIMITED SALES FOR HIS NEGOCIO

Now that you have a great product, or a great deal, you need to commercialize it. Unfortunately, you lack the capital to do that successfully that way it is than you he needs to find cheap or cheap forms to commercialize his business. Top-quality one the fact that you forge marketing out there is You Tubo. The advantage, the TV is free to send videos!

So how the can that you create unlimited sales for your business using Its Tube?

In the past, people relied on revisions, broadcasts, newspapers, television, ads fences, and ads of the radio leading to the people to his business and that way making sales. However, today nearly everybody uses the Internet. Consequently, the marketing of the Internet is important every bit as like some other type of commercializing tactics perhaps even more important. The majority of business today have taxi stands Webes, as well. If you are going to sell something then you need to create your taxi stand professional Web to keep up with the times.

You can create a marketing video and then the TV is able to send it Tube to you itself. Using the marketing characteristics on the premises Web per se, you can commercialize it for another one to You the users of the Tube, as well as they label as use and the categories to simplify your video for the discovery stops out of users also.

Besides, you can use the link than You the Tube creates and your marketing video in its place can actually embed Web or can take your personal daily newspaper in the Internet. There it is not at all complicated to learn here. You can actually make the solidum with a couple of clicks of a button simply.

Having an on-line presence like this you Web will be able to draw people from all around the world for its taxi stand. You can catch up with an a lot audience more broad than what you could with your local newspaper. **So what do you need to make this?**

Basically, you need a video camera, a good microphone, a little bit of knowledge of the computer, and any creativity. Absolutely, you also need a good product, commercial, or the services to promote, as well.

You should try to find some creative angle when creating his to You the marketing video Tube. You do not want to make an infomercial, or any kind of publicity typical ad. People do not make a pass at you to observe standard publicities. Help to be creative and impartial to find some sort of appliance.

Most of all, do not forget to mention his business name, his taxi stand's address Web, and any other pertinent information that will take to his own taxi stand Web to the visits.

SEEING YOUR MARKETING VIDEO IN YOU TUBE

Creating a great marketing video and TV to send that for You the Tube is a part of the process of making the taxi stand simply a wonderful effect for its business or product gives Web. You then have to insure that people actually know that you are out there. After all, You that the Tube has more than 20 million spectators every month. You have to find a little very to stand out of all others.

SO HOW DO YOU OBTAIN YOUR MARKETING VIDEO DID YOU SEE IN YOU ANY TUBE?

Insure that people find our taxi stand Web. If you have a taxi stand I exteriorize Web, and it will implicate that you make, you or can conduct the people to his the Tube videotapes thereof to You, or you can embed your video in its place Web in yourself without sending people to you the Tube to observe it. One way or another, the people in its place need Web seeing their video. In like manner, the people in You Tube the fact that they observe their marketing video should be able to find its taxi stand I exteriorize Web. Make certain that you include a taxi stand's address Web that conducts the people for your taxi stand. In another way, they have just observed a great video but they have not even the faintest idea how to contact him or buying the product that they have just to see. You can include the address in the video same, but also he can make sure that you have your URL in your profile, as well.

Become implicated in it You the community Tube. Something like other social taxi stands of benefit, You the Tube has an active community. Do not forget to participate in groups, creating your group, reacting to the videos, sending e-mails and bulletins outside, and generally making oneself known. Her your presence is more strongly, the more people will observe their videos and will hopefully understand for your taxi stand Web.

Choose the correct key words. After you beech TV once his video was sent, you he will need to choose categories and labels. This is very important. Why? Because it is how people will find their video. Simply do not use aleatory words that they do not have a lot to make with your video. In the meantime the remaining of the I to conduct traffic toward that, you also want to conduct the correct traffic.

Remember your audience. People do not make a pass at you to search skilfully, polished videos. Consequently, you do not need to go out and to spend thousands and thousands of dollars to make your video. Professional should be seen, but you do not have look as if you spent a significant amount of money to make it.

CHOOSE YOUR IMPORTANT STEP NICHE AN IN HIS TO YOU THE TUBE'S MARKETING VIDEO

When you get ready in order that one You tell it of the Tubo they commercialize their business, their services, or products, one of the most important things you can make you should choose the correct niche. Why? Because you can help him with marketing you have Tube in mind even inside You.

You would be able to think that you do not want to limit yourself over there simply choosing a kind of niche.

However, think about that like being a little fish at a big pond if you only go with The Standard account. Embracing each other below your niche, you have a better chance of being our of the crowd. You also help to populate discovery. Once they have found you, you will have more clicks in your videos and then hopefully, more clicks for your taxi stand I exteriorize Web.

Absolutely, you only can always go with a standard account. However, if you commercialize something specific then you have felt to make too much and choosing one of the other options. Let's look them straight in the face ...

A Guru's Account. If you are an expert at home and your videos go to show that then you should sign up for the Guru's account. With the Guru's account you he can have links for his others web sites of his page of the profile, as well as a logo.

A Director Account. Are you an edifying Spielberg? If so, back then you should consider a Director account that is a good option if you the TV sends its own videos that you has made itself to you yourself to present its creativity.

A Comedian's Account. A lot of comedians get ready in order that You count of the Tube have exposition. You can also promote your standing act, public program of television of access, or even his they promote their DCs. Besides, with this sort of account you also he can list upcoming shows also.

You tell her The ambitious musicians about the Musician of the 4.A. they should choose this option. With a musician's account, you can promote your music with You Tubo. You he will be able to choose his kind of music, making a logo, show than his executed excursion, and even giving him people lace them in the ones that they can buy his CDs in.

If you decide later that you want to choose a niche and not only being faithful to the Standard then you can do that, as well. Simply go to your Y channel's page of information change your type of the account.

BELIEVE HIM AND CUSTOMIZE YOURS YOU THE CANAL OF THE TUBE TO COMMERCIALIZE HIS BUSINESS

If you consider yourself to use his Tube in order to commercialize his business, product, or services then the first thing that you need to make is creating and making your canal to order. This is not in reality so tough literally. In fact, although it is very important, the taxi stand Web per se the work makes it more than for you.

So why should you create you yours You the Tube's canal?

Once you have created a canal, you the TV is able to send its videos. Not only that, but you will have a presence on the premises Web. You will go from being a very visit in between million for a real contributor. This will let you interact inside it You community of the Tube, some of your inhouse than using commercializes tactics, and even embedding the videos than you the TV sends for its taxi stand Web free. You only cannot find a better marketing reason than that.

How do you create you yours You the Tube's canal?

Actually, when you apply for a history, the canal is right now tightly there for you, waiting. You are just to you to make it his. You can add up any personal information about yourself, or your company, as well as include your taxi stand's address Web and another important information. Besides, you can also show your favorite videos not made by you either or somebody else. **What do a certain amount of the other advantages create one of in relation to make your canal to order?**

You will have a profile with your URL. You will also get only You URL of the Tube that you can use in other social taxi stands of benefit, or your taxi stand Web, in order to conduct traffic stops his to You the Tube's videos.

You he can accustom various the fact that the shows of the Tube like it sends an email, bulletins, groups To You, and other social public services to associate with other users, to promote his videos, or for learn the valuable information so that it is referred to how making his marketing videos **better.**

 Do I have to be erudition of the Internet for TV to send Tube to You?

Of course not. In fact, once your device is caused to become addicted to its computer, you only have than TV sending the video of the same mode than you the TV would send its digital pictures. Once it has been TV send, You the Tubo will do the rest of work. You have simply to choose categories and the labels that you consider they square their marketing video. Absolutely, to begin with, you have to create a great marketing video, as well.

PROMOTE YOUR BUSINESS WITH THESE 5 TO WITH YOU THE TUBE COMMERCIALIZING STRATEGIES

You the Tube the father is about to promote, but you need to do him the right way. It is important to look in

You the Tube like the destination's taxi stand instead of like a taxi stand of search. That that you take than in consideration, back then you will use his Tube like a supplement for your marketing and the promotion of your product and the business, not like your global plan of marketing. Why?

Simply put, because there are thousands and thousands of videos out there. Really. The odds of their video being seen by an aleatory person are very good. Yes, you he can use to have good labels and categories and that will help his video to be located, but that would be able to take time.

Instead, it is much better to create a taxi stand I exteriorize Web, even a blog, and then getting drugs his to You the Tube's video. That way, the people that are interested in right now your product will be able to see a video about that to help to supplement the information that you right now have supplied. Here there are 5 pieces of advice more than they will help to enter promoting your business or the product with You Tubo. The use your sent TV You the Tube videotapes in its company's blog. You also can use it at your company the page MySpace of page or Facebook, as well as on the premises Web per se.

The same good-looking thing for Gorjeo. Do not underestimate the value of Twitter these days. Make sure that your bringing ups to date you include links to his to You the taxi stand of the Tube.

The use his You the Tubo directs URL to any e-mails that go outside that you send. Make out part of your signature so so whoever you send them to, they will be able to see their link. Make this for both commercial and personal e-mails, but make sure that the signature is not needlessly big. That can do dumb comments.

Convince an important blogger or communal group to use your video. For example, if your local community has an on-line newsletter and you they announce their business with them, they add you their video to that or a link to the video in its place. Besides, ask to them about mailing a link for your video in its place, as well.

Use the video or the video link in so many pertinent areas like you be able. Earn plus placing them on some crucial areas where you will put him to than an audience aimed at specific areas they to mail them everywhere you he can and nobody that has really interest does not fit. Relevance is the key here.

USING VIRAL CONTENTS CREATING HIS PERFECT TO YOU THE TUBE'S MARKETING VIDEO

You want to use his Tube for the marketing of his business, service, do I lay siege to Web, or product? You sure make! By this time you know than You the Tube can be an energetic location to promote its business, competition creating some big videos that can lead traffic toward its taxi stand Web.

So how do you take care of creating for oneself his perfect You the marketing of the Tube do you videotape for his business?

First, know that the on-line video makes him to have rules. This means that you do not make a film, Mr. Spielberg. You do not want your video to be for a long time and dragging. For that reason, it is better to start with a paper. Trim glass out of any unnecessary information. Nobody wants to hear you talking on and on. Does he remember at school when you wrote and did they tell you worth more to come out to light and no saying? The form that goes when you believe is that one his perfect to You the marketing video Tube.

Try to maintain the video per se below five minutes in length. Do you think that that is short? All right, consider the communis advertisement than the race at about 45 seconds. Destiny, while we are on the subject of publicity ads ...

Remember your on-line video is not an advertisement. Although it is a publicity in the fact that you are trying to take to the people technically to buy something in the long run, what's typical you the Tube videotapes he entertains, educate, or reveal information - it is wanted to say -. So you do not negotiate that like an infomercial delayed by night.

If your video happens to be longer for some reason, this can take place in educational videos where you teach somebody how to make out of something like part your marketing tactics, to consider to resolve it into segments. Later, you can combine the segments in a playlist. Why should you make this? Because his audience then will be able to jump over itself in front, or back, for the parts that they want to see.

After all, if they know exactly that they are looking for, they do not want to sit however several minutes of something in the ones that are not interested simply to lay eggs for that matter. In fact, they will not probably make it. Instead, only they will get off the video.

One of the best forms that you can take care of creating yourself his perfect You something that is educational should make the Tube's marketing videos. Show your audience how to make something that is related to your product or business. The people like to learn things. Then, at the end of the video, address Web to your siege. This is an a lot less invasive form of publicity.

YOU PIPE TO COMMERCIALIZE TACTICSES: ARE THESE PRODUCTS OR TRÁCALAS HELPFUL?

Now that creating what's perfect You the marketing video Tube is popular for small business like a form to promote his produces or your web sites, a lot of companies have begun to sell books, DVDs, and CDs put the sight in trying to teach to you how doing you the right way. However, these marketing tacticses are helpful, Or simply any other way for people making money?

What Companies' offer:

Basically, the various companies that are out there pawning information what one refers in to how making what's perfect You video the marketing Tube says than teach how not only creating the video per se, but making million people to observe it. What else do they make an offer?

How creating them yours participative video web sites

How increasing your sales and your marketing efforts uncontrollably

How using for how efficaciously video sharing taxi stands Webes

The secrets to choose big key words to label his videos with

How to build your community of the video of the niche in YouTube with the characteristic of groups

How using videos like a device of sales in its place company's Web

These,, are of course some things that the greater part of these companies promise simply.

The Information Is Helpful:

Sure, you are too how-to. Everything that you need to know are those so that he refers to create to create for himself and to promote his You the marketing of the Tube videotapes. The piece of advice would have too much good consequences then somebody that is not really certain than what they are making.

This is The Whole Swindle:

In a way, that the class of it is. After all, although you will take some time and effort, everything that information right now can be found free in the internet. Simply doing a search easy in You pieces of advice of the Tube, including in his taxi stand Web, you he can find his answers for everything the above-cited questions. Consequently, although the information so many of the these products make an offer you are helpful, you are not something for what you necessarily should pay.

Is it the Information in reality so Easy for the Discovery?:

All right, you are going to take some time and effort. Still, you are out there. There is hundreds of free goods that you applied over yourself creating yours for oneself You marketing videos Tube, pieces of advice so that you make a good video, and even more revenues in relation to commercialize them in the best way form. Simply doing a fast search you will produce hundreds. However, if you do not want to experience everything that work, back then feel free to spend the money.

10 PIECES OF ADVICE TO USE TUBE FOR YOUR MARKETING VIDEO

You the Tube can be a great form to commercialize its product or business. However, there is more for You the Tube than simply TV sending your video and hoping that people will observe it. You have to commercialize your marketing video also! The following is a list of 10 pieces of advice that will help you if you use You the Tube to commercialize purposes.

Choose your niche. When you apply for a history, you need to choose your niche. If you want to promote your music, back then you need account to a Musician. If you promote his then you need a Comedian's account of foot. However, if you are an expert at home and you want to promote your services back then you should consider him a Guru counts. Earn plus embracing each other below his field to be found easier.

Make a playlist. This is good for the promotional value. You can include the somebody else's videos also, or simply his. This is in good individual if you have long videos and needs to some of the clips trim glass down.

Choose his labels and categories wisely. Your labels, as well as the categories that you choose your videos in them that to be, they are more important that you think. These are the things that people will use to find him. Using a less popular category would be able to help you to find a bigger audience ever since your competition is smaller.

Leave the answers to the somebody else's videos. Being a presence, more you would be able to examine his people.

Use the Active characteristic of Uso Enjoyed In Common to quit to the people to see what videos that you observe. When somebody sees that you observe to the same thing like them, they would be able to click on their profile for curiosity.

Create your canal. This finishes when you get ready. Insure that you have mailed your taxi stand's address Web in order that people can find you.

Get mixed up in the community. Send e-mails and bulletins to require the people to visit your videos outside. Do not send unsolicited emails, however.

Embed your videos in its place Web. Simply do not show them in You Tube Use they in your taxi stand Web also.

A group believes, or only deliver yours. Having the like-minded people side by side, you believe a bigger audience.

The check mark his You the URL of the Tube divides of its signature every time that you send e-mails outside for the customers or even friends.

FACEBOOK FAN PAGE IOTS AND TRICKS

Contents

JUAN GOMEZ

10 Pieces Of Advice for Increase I
The best Methods stops Inside
How Bringing Up Your Faceb
5 Things You Would Owe Respect to
How Bringing Up Your Faceb
The Tricks To Grow Your Fa
How You Can Grow Your Page
How stops Successfully Of
4 Forms You Dog Increas

USING ADS TO BRING UP YOUR FACEBOOK TO FACEBOOK PAGE FANS

One of the easiest ways to increase your pleasures Facebook is through Facebook Ads's use, which one lets him aim at him the demographic characteristics specific, which means that you will let him bring the traffic that you desire for your page.

Do not mix up Facebook Ads with Anuncios Google, because they are not all the same. Search the Internet using Google that Ads will put of manifesto when a person looks for her key word actively (s). They will usually want to know what you offer at that time, that you elicit a click that has importance for his search.

Facebook Ads do not work that way. A Facebook Ad puts of manifesto when a person browses his News Is Fed that way it is that they do not probably have any aims to buy of yours at that time. That means that you should offer incentives to conduct clicks in the Facebook Ad using one of the three methods – coupons, competitions, or electronic books.

These ads Facebooks they let you aim at him those that do not have right now pleasures your page. You even can include an analogous button well in your ad. You can use the basic format (insert what they will receive). You can conduct Pleasures based in the incentive. There are a few that you can use here:

I eat we and lead to his Free Guía to Bring Up His Facebook Business
I eat we to serve the ball one the % the coupon's 20 Exclusivo
I eat we to earn $200's marketing Consultation
I eat we and the leading to earn a trip for Vegas – the tie every 3 months

Facebook Ads is also a lot more affordable than Anuncios Google. It wants to say that even if you have a budget you can take advantage under of Facebook Ads. Si you want to Facebook Ads know more about using and how for the plan your campaign Facebook Ad, Facebook you have a core section in relation to establish his campaign form, so.

Your intention with its Facebook Page is bringing up its Likes and its base of the agreement easy to wiggle out of. Making that that you need taking advantage with what's a lot of equips that with tools you can help him to make a powerful Facebook Ad.

Ads are Facebook quiet of the most misunderstood opportunities to bring up your Facebook Page and to increase your traffic aimed at specific areas and your pleasures. The rest is your decision. With the so captivating use of firm poles your followers you can increase your reach further on and can continue bringing up your Page.

THE PIECES OF ADVICE FOR CREATE FACEBOOK TO YOU POSTS THAT HE IS NICE

If you he wants to grow his agreement easy to wiggle out of's base and to increase his pleasures, you he is going to need to have poles for his page that is interesting and keeps his visitors wanting to return. There is here 5 pieces of advice to create poles Facebook that they enter into a contract.

The #1's Copy of Use, the Images and Videos That It Is Nice

Photos and the videos that it is media-rich you will have attention and they will help your message to seem to be further at a Newsworthy fodder.

The way of life and the inspirational images are nice always. The smart owners Page they hurry up to take advantage of these images, because they understand that they do not have to have importance for the product service that you offer yourself to be relevant for your agreement easy to wiggle outs of. These fans then will share these poles with their friends and that provides you with more reach and another opportunity turning around his ' Pleasures.' The *'s images/photos Share of your products with your customers enjoying them.

The best poles are in between 100 and 250 characters – shortie and he has the greater part of attention for the point.

The part of the #2 and the Discounts Promote and the promotions That Exclusiva is
Offer one in good reality to his visits reward or negotiate to keep applicants. You can increase your sales and can increase the size of your followers with this technique.
Bargain 1 puts 1 free he seems to be a very popular promotion and that way also it is when you he gives things as a present free.
In order to increase the commitment of your visits, make sure that you have a call of the clearing to make going.

The Settling-Down of the #3 and the Punctuality
When your poles are related with that they are thinking at the time, like the holidays or a present-day sporting event, your audience he is a lot more probable to enter into a contract
The punctuality in answering you any it is poles that have a comment in them also important. While you faster are for answering your agreement easy to wiggle outs of what's more probably they will continue that one entering into a contract to you.

The Traffic of Walk in Car of the #4 for Your Website With Links
Poles Link they have an area that it is bigger pray and that Web helps people to find its taxi stand, right over there increasing his traffic.
Use poles of the link to take to your taxi stand Web to people Poles Link now they have a bigger, capable area to do click that helps to take to their taxi stand Web to people. Take the title, image and description, which comes from the URL, and make him to order.

Bring these 4 pieces of advice into play and observe your agreement easy to wiggle outs of to grow.

DEVELOP YOUR AGREEMENT EASY TO WIGGLE OUTS OF OF THE PAGE OF THE FACEBOOK

Your agreement easy to wiggle outs of are the heart for their Facebook Page having success. Except building those fans and 'De Likes can be a challenge really. Let's look in 5 tricks to bring up your Facebook Page Fans.

The media of Social Gathering of Use of the #1 of Trick
The use of media social canals like LinkedIn, the + Google or the Chirp it is a great form to encourage the people to Facebook to visit his page. These are free you forge the marketing that you should take advantage of. In addition to rectilinear poles, he makes sure that you occasionally cross pole of one to the other one. The chirp only allows 140 characters so the good use of the their check mark.

The Advantage of the photo of the #2 of Trick of Public Events
Often overlooked, still an energetic tool that a great form to spread the word can be. If you are performing the public speaking is sure you include your URL Facebook Page on the slide show as you make it easy that they associate people. If you attend link in net to meetings this is quite a while to encourage the members to Taste his Facebook Page and becoming agree-

ment easy to wiggle outs of.

The Page of the Agreement Easy To Wiggle Out Of of the #3 of
Trick on Fridays
In Facebook, there are Pages than the host Fan Page Viernes's
events. If you participate, you will be encouraged to stop by
the page in a specific date to initiate your business all over the
world that participates and then will label as your page in the
pole. The idea is than you he will work through all the comments and he will be pleasing to each of the participating pages
than He Will Like his page in the turn. A word of warning.
Only take part in local events, because if you land up with a
lot of international agreement easy to wiggle outs of, actually
EdgeRank would be able to decrease his punctuation. Besides, if
the other ones hide their fodder of news themselves you travel
quickly because only they wanted your Como and the applicants are not in their business, would be able to hurt you.

The #4 of Trick Encourage Check Ins in Your Facebook Page
For somebody that you have a brick and the mortar business,
you should habilitate Facebook checks ins in his page, and then
you remind him to customers of getting registered when they
are in their facilities. You even can include an incentive as offering a discount.

The Use of the check mark of the #5 of Trick of Signposting
When customers visit their brick and they join the business
with mortar, you can create signposting for in your store that
lets the customers To Like Him his page using a message text.
You would look at your signposting something like this. "I eat
the text (the name of the insert Facebook Page) for 34587. Try
this in your cellular phone first before you commit your budget
ad hoc. You can also develop signposting that includes your social media's icons.

These 5 tricks work big growing your Facebook Page unfolds.

DEVELOP YOUR PLEASURES OF THE FACEBOOK WITH THESE 5 PIECES OF ADVICE

Facebook is a location where conversations take place. You talk to your fans in your Facebook Page or do do him conversation in them? The number of agreement easy to wiggle outs of that you have is a quite good reference stops how you try of your agreement easy to wiggle outs of. What's more you talk to your fans the top that your number of agreement easy to wiggle outs of will be. Use profitably your social space understanding he and you will see your Facebook Page that Pleasures continue bringing up. There are 5 pieces of advice to help you to bring up his Facebook Likes here.

1. Talk back to Your Fans – You mail a comment, back then a fan comments on the pole, and you need to answer that comment. Ideally, what you want to achieve is conversation that goes back and forth between you and his agreement easy to wiggle out of (s). The more agreement easy to wiggle outs of that participate the best. Leaving your agreement easy to wiggle outs of to feel a conversation they are taking place that they have a better chance of participating. If you post and a fan

makes comments and you do not recoil the conversation dies down and the reach subsides with her. 2. Make sure that there is very much Photos and Videos Mailed – People prefer photos on texts. Make your Facebook Page visually appealing using graphics, photos and videos. This will extract the interest of his agreement easy to wiggle outs of and they are a lot more probable to share photos, graphics and videos than text, which in turn extends his reach.

Choose the Chronological Line's Best Photo – The last format Facebook – the Timeline's page is either hated or dear. Request that you post a horizontal conspicuous image I join with a more little detailed shot that is order of the cards. This is a good location for her logo. Make sure his photos they are comfortable and happy. You are great if they interact or they tap into their agreement easy to wiggle outs of.

Take advantage of the Social Tabs – it is a good idea crossing over some others promote media social pages that you have. You he can add up you label for Google +, I Chirp, Pinterest, etcetera.

Post Regularly – Your fees are Facebook hour and the printed goods go out of style. His poles are grouped monthly that way it is that his fans can easily scroll down their page and they can also see how often you post every month. That way than if you only travel quickly 7 times on the end of week and then not again even the following weekend his agreement easy to wiggle outs of he goes in order to lose interest and the potential new agreement easy to wiggle outs of are not going to enthuse themselves also about tasting their page. It is very important that you destine regularly to generate interest.

THE TOP SECRET OVERTURNS TO HELP A SUCCESSFUL TO RUN FAN ITSELF PAGE

There are Facebook sends to call and is " Facebook Pages." Some pages are just there. They exist, they are boring and they do nothing to want their audience to become a. Other pages have crying factor. They are attractive, they offer great value and the audience is sucked in. The kind of Facebook Page do you have? There are some top-secret pieces of advice to help you to run a page hit of the agreement easy to wiggle out of that not only brings the people to his page here, but you help they develop their agreement easy to wiggle outs of and pleasures.

Start with a Cover's Incredible Photo
The image at the top of its page can pull you. He can perceive his imagination and it can lead you to some beautiful spot. Make sure that you understand I join the importance of your photo of the cover that you choose and that you will work for of yours. There are a lot of on-line resources to help you with this.

Create an Image of the Profile That is unique
What one refers to profiling pictures in, we tend to glue our picture same up there and that's that. But there is so much value in using an only image of the profile your audience will remember with or she will associate with. Begin with defining what a your business approximately. Then try to create an image that

is epoch-making and creates intense branding. Hire a visual art-
ist if you need.   It is worthwhile!

Make good use of the Facebook Page APPs
Facebook offers you some big application softwares, so you
mark it sure to explore them and to do use thereof. Add to any
that it is appropriate. Do not be frightening to do use of varied.
You will help to increase the size of his spectators along with
his pleasures.

The Regular Customer of the Pole and the Captivating Poles
It is not quite good to create a pole sometimes. You need to
have normal poles every day in order that you show up in the
newsworthy fodders and in order that your fans look forward
to their poles and be ready to read and sharing those poles. Besides, you need to make sure that you have to link poles in order
that they throw clubs to their fans to make comments and to
participate of a debate. This will help to increase his reach.

Strongly Call Action
He has a lot of importance than his page Facebook have an
intense call to make going, because without her what it is sup-
posed that they make will not know his visits. The friends of
selling price to click on the LIKE button in an evident and suc-
cinct form that place does not let to the blunders.

THE KEY A BASE OF THE AGREEMENT EASY TO WIGGLE OUT OF IN FACEBOOK PAGES QUE IS COMPROMISED FOR FINCAR

To grow your agreement easy to wiggle out of's base is one of its Facebook Page's important parts but which one is important every bit as it is having agreement easy to wiggle outs of that they will hire in his page. This means that you will have agreement easy to wiggle outs of that they will like his page, the comment in poles and part travels quickly because they want, no because they are being tempted to for a reward like a coupon or free giveaway. That the bird call returns to with such than the good contents.

The good Content?
The good contents will deduct advantage from life, interests and alive situations of its target market. It can be related to everyday life and you should provoke a personal answer immediately. He relates to each other with all kinds of contents,

ask for users' opinion, and he says to puncture him stories. What you make is creating an attitude of the village square where users get together to socialize themselves and finding something interesting to enter into a contract to like disposed people.

If you he is in doubt still of how creating strongly contained, back then blame a look in some of the Facebook that they created pages and headed by large business organizations like Proctor and the Play.

You he can create this sort of contents defining his target market and then determining what pertinent themes are for that marketplace. Then believe contained of the themed that you can program in order that you have constant poles going out to your users. You can use some of the options of Facebook, like ads Facebook to aim at your audience and to expand your reach through your poles.

Making sure that you are blank and having the reach you go of, to you they should use Facebook Page Analytics to analyze their poles. This can provide you with sensible information that will let you to be able to reform decisions he related with his poles and his future poles that you would be able to make.

There is a lot of forms that you can build your fan they base that actually you will not help his business prosper, so maintenance that in mind. However, taking his time to bring you wrote him down to traffic for your Facebook Page and growing a pertinent base of the agreement easy to wiggle out of that you can enjoy of the complete benefits of the work you lay eggs in this.

To the long term that your intention is continuing growing your fans of across He Likes It and that they are in love by what you offer so much so that they tell their friends that they tell the turn to their friends and that reach you can continue increasing and growing, offering you a marketing opportunity very powerful.

AGREEMENT EASY TO WIGGLE OUTS OF AND PLEASURES

Growing your Facebook unfolds and pleasures can be a challenge. In fact, the appearance of a little bit of a daunting task would be able to have enough money for a certain amount. The good news that he does not have to obfuscate. Let's consider two of the best forms to develop his agreement easy to wiggle outs of and pleasures.

The #1 of Method Grow Your Facebook Fans and Pleasures with Competitions
This is easy one of the methods to excite the people about his page and to carry the new agreement easy to wiggle outs of to his page. The attraction of earning the big reward means that your target market is going to appear, doing click Like, and becoming an agreement easy to wiggle out of in your page.

How Bringing People Que Missing To Introduce Your Competition for Como Your Page and Convertido in an Agreement Easy To Wiggle Out Of that there is a number of party 3 combat the applications you can elect between, like Wishpond they have an useful characteristic, which is designated Like Portón, designed to recast the doorway page of competition after Tasting the Facebook Page.

As the Gate is an image that has text that tells the visitor that they have Like the page elks of you can agree to the fantastic competition. Once Likes Them it the application software automatically you charge the entrance predetermined for the page competition or the one that votes where the user between his competition.

To Método Grow's #2 Your Facebook Fans and Gustos With They Like Gated Coupons
Coupons are an excellent promotion that is very received. Make a coupon even stops so little like 10 percent completely gives you incentive of visits to buy its product while you manage to walk off with your fairly unhurt outer edges. The best form to use coupons is in order that you make them accomplish any action in order that they can come over the coupon but that should not be tough or consuming.

There is Aplicaciones's number of the Coupon that they provide to create the Gate's coupon, with the codes of the coupon incorporated to a Facebook Como. A decent Application Software of the Coupon gives facilities in order that you design your right of coupons in Facebook. When the coupon is correct forward, Facebook that you are also further easy to share it.

Do not forget to include your call to make going with all your marketing Facebook Page to insure you grow your agreement easy to wiggle outs of and the way of pleasures that you want. The blunder that owners Page do and what then you have verificative is is verificative you are you do the whole hard work and you do not have the results that you want.

4 TECHNIQUES TO ENLARGE LIKES TO YOUR FACEBOOK

So that it is referred to implementing media social strategies, Facebook is a great location to throw the net as it is than have it more than users. However, if you thought that the publication for Facebook sometimes is enough, you would be wrong. Using that strategy is going to have babe of blowout instead of growing. Let's look in 4 technicians To Increase your Facebook Likes and developing your agreement easy to wiggle outs of.

#1. Label him as Yourself in Your Photos
This technique is so give-away to accustom that you will ask yourself why you did not use it sooner. Of today make sure that in each very photo that you raise in your Facebook Page you label as yourself yourself in each very photo. This is smart because if your contents is good and his shareable back then you will appear in the fodders of news of other ones. When he joins of the stocks of his agreement easy to wiggle out of than that, his joint agreement easy to wiggle out of back then is going to be connected at the section shared in addition to the image.

The #2 Create Content Que is Shareable
The good contents is great, but the great contents is major. It is very important to have contents that is shareable. This means that your contents is as good that your audience only does not want to taste it, they want to share it with their friends. The contents that your agreement easy to wiggle outs of share in is really part of your on-line identity. You say to the other

ones what they like it and who they are. In this case also show support for you. When the contents is shareable, it increases his because you expose his name to more people, putting your check mark foremost part of those that your agreement easy to wiggle outs of are not at present out there into.

The #3 Remember for Rest Consistent
You do not want to develop remaining to get boring. You do not want to have a week with a big peak and back then your page puts drum of buzz loused up to the following big peak. This type of inconsistency will have people leaving its page. Instead consistently hire your audience that way it is that can depend of yours.

The Wrist Watch of the #4 Your Good Timing
If you want the greater part of people to see their poles, back then you need to post when most people are in Facebook. Mornings and afternoons are generally more convenient, but for supposition that you will need to determine what's more convenient for your audience. You perhaps cater to an international market that way it is that you will need to serve the ball in definite the best time to post locally to attain that market. Do not be frightening to experience to see discovery the best time for your poles.

BETTER THE CONSTANT SECRETS TO BRING UP YOUR FACEBOOK PAGE FANS

If you have created a Facebook Page, your following intention is increasing your Pleasures and fanning base. There are a lot of forms to make this and we want to share some of the best constant secrets to develop his agreement easy to wiggle outs of Facebook Page.

Train a character for your audience. Some business have a description of so that your ideal lover looks alike. This can help you to visualize his communication and so that your poles should look alike in Facebook.
Install an Application Software of Compromiso in your Facebook Page. There are a lot of big application softwares on the market that can help to achieve it this like Booshaka or Agreement Easy To Wiggle Out Of of the Week.
Facebook has imposed some restrictions so that you are allowed to embrace your new images of the cover permission to embrace your new images her cover, but only applies over himself the outstanding pages not for your personal profile, so you would be able to consider yourself to bring a commercial aspect into your personal timeline through your image of the cover.
If you have several page admins, take advantage of the last adjustments of the admin of the page than the rents that you assign him to the authority each person. Go to his Admin Panel

then Edite to Page where of the drop-down menu than you Admin Roles selects. Once you will see the Perfil Pic of every Admin with your present-day paper in the page. In order to change your present-day paper, only doing click in the down arrow to the right of the present-day title of paper and doing your selection.

Order your keen understandings of the pole in order that you can at a glance see your bringing ups to date more guessed right for. Delve into your keen understandings. In the front page you the time authentic pole will see statistical specific, he will click on the up arrow to order the based bringing ups to date in which they have had it more than commitments. 6. If you accustom Pinterest, why no installing the application software Pinterest in your page Facebook.

Add the Button of message to your Facebook Page that way it is that readers can send an unconscious message. This also lets you recoil privately.

Take advantage of Keen Understandings to learn more about your agreement easy to wiggle outs of, of your age, sexual, where they are of, etcetera. This will help you with his marketing.

These 8 pieces of advice are one a certain amount of the best constant secrets to develop your agreement easy to wiggle outs of Facebook Page. Besides, make sure that you share contained of quality that they will want to share their agreement easy to wiggle outs of with their friends. This will increase his reach and it will help him to develop your agreement easy to wiggle outs of further on.

THE TIPS THAT YOU NEED FOR KNOW BRING UP THEIR BUSINESS PAGE CHILD FACEBOOK

To grow your small business using Facebook can be a very gratifying experience, but also you can be defying and becoming frustrated. Here there are 4 pieces of advice that you need to know to bring up your fans Facebook and pleasures.

The check mark of the #1 An Offer
Promotions, discounts and the free things are all very popular in Facebook. It is a form offering a certain amount of great value to your customers and they are in love by her! You can offer him a discount to somebody that he mentions you in Facebook when they go shopping with you. You may build your reach (pleasures and agreement easy to wiggle outs of) making it simple to your visits to distribute your message beyond your present-day base of the agreement easy to wiggle out of and then making it easy to redeem whatever you have offered them (the discount or the gift).

The #2's Encouragement the Poles That It Is Important
Use Boosted Anuncia in Carteles to help you to increase your audience's reach. Enter the quantity that you are going to set your promotion aside for in and Facebook immediately tells

you how many people that fit will generate. You can write him down within your reach in order that your message is getting to the correct people. For example, you can create poles that catch up with the people close to you. This is an energetic tool that is often overlooked because the users do not understand their complete benefit. It is actual cost and supply a give-away form to expand the reach of his poles. It is important to realize that the tight publication your pole not be enough anymore. You he needs to these additional steps in getting the most out of his poles take long.

Safe The Check Mark of the #3 for Pole Regularly
All day long create a stable current of publication before any big event that you review yourself of rising. This can help his audience to focus. Make sure that you highlight your goods out-standing services, but reach go beyond the self-praise to make good use of your poles to the full. I consider myself to add up poles that will give your audience of more value themselves. When you only drop the mail in your products and bathrooms your audience the bore turns around and it is prone neither recasting your newsworthy fodder or unlike your page. Your audience wanting to learn about it what else behaves badly for the offering contents that you interest him you will make an offer.

The #4 Give Your Page A Facelift
It is time to do some restoration in his page and to add up some value. Make sure that your content information and hours of operation are posted. Update your cover's photo in order that you are present-day and pertinent. Say a little bit about your-self and your business to your audience.

These 4 pieces of advice will help you to bring up their Business Pequeño Facebook Page.

AGREEMENT EASY TO WIGGLE OUTS OF

Facebook is a social platform of the net for the conversation. Are you talking in the mood for your followers in your Facebook Page or talking to them? A good indicator is the number of agreement easy to wiggle outs of that you has. If you want more agreement easy to wiggle outs of than you they have made it, back then it is time to make some changes. You need to understand in order to make good use of your page to the full his ' the social space.' In Facebook there you need to be a lot of chatting back and forth to share information. This includes photos, links, videos and poles. There are 5 here they make a mistake you do proof of impression that the pieces of advice to make sure you understand him correctly.

Do not promote, Depart – His Facebook Page does not exist just to commercialize his products services. If that is all that you make with that, your followers will lose interest quickly. Use your Page to interest the people that use of its products would do services.

Make sure that You, Be Pertinent – Think About his poles, in view of the station, what themes are hot, that gets its name in the newspapers, etcetera. Share links in which his agreement easy to wiggle outs of would be interested and that they want sharing with his friends.

Make Sure Your Poles They Are Interesting – Poles do not have to be newsworthy to be interesting. Your agreement easy to wiggle outs of are not going to be interested in news unless it has importance, but he was interested in finding out about a new product that serves to commercialize that it is relevant. For example, let's say that you run than a medical page, and there is a new treatment of cancer that has proven to promise results. Sharing this information with its agreement easy to wiggle outs of would be wise one way or another interesting, entering into a contract, and pertinent.

Posting About the Competition is all right, Some Times – let's say that a new study is released how interesting you know that you will attract attention. You would be able to be better if you would be able to find your expert to give one's opinion but that is possible not always. You are all right in these cases if you share information of a reputed source even when it is its competition. A common blunder is wanting to avoid just any thing to make with the competition, but sometimes he can ironically be benefitted by his competition instead of putting obstacles to you.

Walk off with Your Fans Hablando – Never underestimate the power of your words. ' What is your opinion?' When you he posts lace them of experts, hot themes or controversial themes, they ask their opinion, their feedback to their audience. Your intention is generating conversation with its agreement easy to wiggle outs of and bringing new agreement easy to wiggle outs of aboard.

These 5 pieces of advice are a great beginning to develop their agreement easy to wiggle outs of Facebook. What are you waiting to?

10 PIECES OF ADVICE TO ENLARGE LIKES TO YOUR FACEBOOK

If you hope to increase your Facebook Like these 10 pieces of advice they are a great location to yack.

1. If you have created a personal page of the profile for your business instead of a commercial page that this is against Facebook's terms and conditions, so you will want to your profile for a commercial new page emigrate. Emigrating lets you make this outside losing all your connections. The tool of migration is Facebook found in https://www.facebook.com/help? Page 213602951994043 2. You should measure your present-day metrics against a benchmark. You will help him this to improve his show in whatever you need to take measurements. First you should register where you at present are. You should also begin to register metrics of the Poste Specific like Gustos's number and the Comments.

Identify an USP for your Page. What does he appreciate are you in good condition to provide to your reading device?

Create a more short custom-made URL for your page. A shorter URL is probable for his visitors to remember and is promoted easily.

Use Keen Understandings to learn what the most popular contents is in its Facebook Page and to learn from where your traffic he originates.

Supply with captions your photos with your marketing message. Add a headline to everything your images/photos providing people with more information about your business. Include a call to make going, a hyper-link, etcetera.

Regularly change your Cover's Image, but walk off with your Perfil Pic the same thing. Every time that you change the cover's Image you become extinguished at the newsworthy fodder that exposition is great.

Make sure that you show your three more important application softwares next to Fotos's application software, an important part is which one to someone's marketing strategy Facebook.

Take the time to create a calendar for your Facebook Page. Planning is very important and planning what you are going to mail about in the advance and then programming than she it can be useful very in your editorial calendar.

Determine what your intention(s) is for using Facebook. Using Facebook just because the competition is, you do not do a quite good reason.

These ten pieces of advice are a great form to start with to increase Pleasures to their Facebook and growing your agreement easy to wiggle out of's base. As well, have in view that your poles are also important, as they will help to improve their reach, which in turn leads to an increment in agreement easy to wiggle outs of.

Your focus should bring up Likes to its Facebook and then walking off with these fans compromised and been interested in in what you have so to speak, eventually leading to sales.

THE BEST METHODS FOR INCREASE FACEBOOK LIKES

Pleasures Facebook are in your page's heart Facebook. You want to build your fans, but you also want those agreement easy to wiggle outs of to be relevant! So we consider the best methods to increase pleasures Facebook.

Incremento's Facebook of Método's #1 Likes To Use Competitions

One of the methods given as a present to be interesting to you to people and to walk away with them you are to his page using competitions. The people like the free goods and so you can see why offering something free you would increase new agreement easy to wiggle outs of for his page especially when the condition to introduce the competition is that you should like the page first. The attraction of conquering a reward helps you to aim you at its market and to grow your pleasures.

To Método Grow's #2 Your Facebook Fans and Gustos With They Like Gated Coupons

Coupons are another great form for to promote your page Facebook. The coupon does not have to be big. You can be so little like 10 % out of a purchase. It is a great form providing an incentive to buy the product (s) that you offer to your audience and that you can still hold your profit margins looking quite healthy.

Incremento's Facebook of Método's #3 Likes To Use Electronic Books

At the mercy of your industry, education can be a better incentive than even offerer a reward or a discount. This is especially true with companies B2B that they like to receive electronic free books or the blank papers that supply themselves of information and the tools to help them to grow his business. This is a great form to conduct large numbers of visits toward her page and to increase her agreement easy to wiggle outs of significantly. You deal with an audience aimed at specific areas, which is what you want exactly.

If you are not certain that your electronic books should be near consider that your business is near and that you can share with your prospective clients that you will be useful and will cause them to become addicted to in what you have to offer. Your electronic book should also include that an intense call to get that going has the reader wanting to know more and wanting to take advantage of the service (s) you the offer.

If you he wants to maximize his reach in promoting his offers, consider yourself to take advantage of ads Facebook, which ones cost too little and leave easily to take aim to him to his marketplace to maximize his benefits. These ads are unlike the Anuncios Google so they do not confuse themselves. You can learn more about Facebook Ads below the how-to section in Facebook.

The #4 of Method Provide Useful and Engaging Content
In addition to offer coupons or they insure free things that the contents that is in his page is useful, interesting and captivating. By his visits have a better chance of making comments and to strike up a conversation. In turn, those conversations become joint and that propagates its reach.

HOW BRINGING UP YOUR FACEBOOK FANS IN YOUR PAGE

Facebook has changed the form that we grew to our business. Your Facebook Business Page is a great form to put all together an audience aimed at specific areas. Your intention is developing your agreement easy to wiggle outs of or Pleasures, but re-membering that you only do not want somebody clicking on something similar; You want to bring for your page that that services have a genuine interest in their products. While they will be anyone of Pleasures they are not going to grow anyone of Pleasures to their business. There is here some strategies to develop your agreement easy to wiggle outs of Facebook in your Page

Using your Facebook Page like a location for your agreement easy to wiggle outs of to meet be father, but you will want to make sure that your poles are interesting and entering into a contract. Your followers will put into the good poles making comments and contratándose to each other, along with shar-ing these poles for the not much followers, those who in turn would be able to find it being interesting to you and They Would Be Able To Like his Page.
Invite a couple of others aboard like Admin of your Page. Then they can advise it to for their friends and your reach can in-crease. Besides, having more than what a white-collar worker can offer different perspectives, that you can help to maintain the page being interesting to you. You can also make somebody react to the poles and the most efficient comments. As your

page grows, the more admins that you should consider oneself to have.

Encourage his visits to mail pictures in his wall, that will help to his page Facebook to show up in Noticia's Fodder. Facebook that users are in love for imagine, so take advantage of them and encourage his followers to openly sharing his photos.

The inspirational images are very received. In fact, they are one of the most popular stocks in Facebook so safe check mark to include them in his Facebook Page.

If you he has business to a Brick and Mortero, you he can use his printed goods means of communication to promote Pleasures for the special deals and the discounts. You can also take advantage of Facebook Offers.

If you have a big enlisted e-mail, you can suggest for those in your list that You Taste your Facebook Page. You would also be able to tell your Gorjeo's followers that they drop in and Like Them your page.

Take advantage of Facebook Ads, that he is easy to establish itself and very affordable. It is a great form to aim at him his traffic and bringing more 'Pleasures.'

These five give-away things can help him to bring up their Facebook Page. Get ready to have a good time of more pleasures and agreement easy to wiggle outs of and building your business.

5 THINGS THAT YOU SHOULD ADD HIM TO YOUR FACEBOOK FAN PAGE

One of the growth of taxi stands keeps on being Facebook more than the media social popular in thousands of users one day. It does not take a lot of effort to recognize his influence for all these users' vast track record, and any company, not taking into account the size and product will be able to promote her make and creating familiarity of the product, in the meantime always strengthening prospective clients. It is easy to create a page Facebook, what many are not in the know of that creating a page is Facebook that an agreement easy to wiggle out of's firm base easily collects pleasures and farm, it is a daunting task.

When a visitor makes it to his page Facebook, the majority will give a click either his information or wall, and if they do not find anything that you perceived your interest that they will simply leave their page. When a visit likes his page, it is for his advantage, because this new agreement easy to wiggle out of will be updated sometimes with things that you publish.

You could have found pages in Facebook that they are so well-done that you ask how it was possible. The great news! There are 5 things that you need to know of your Facebook here they fan page.

The #1 Embed YouTube Video
Facebook does not leave you instantly to run twinkle. You have to throw it using a click on an image, so you need an image every time that you raise a video in Facebook. You can put your URL with a custom picture.

#2 Product Making Comments
If you want to establish a little store in your commercial page Facebook, this characteristic is excellent. You have each product liked and back then made comments be more than enough.

The #3 Insert Flash Content
If you Facebook with files wants to make to order his agreement easy to wiggle out of's pages of the twinkle for the headline or at the photo's gallery. If you are going to embed twinkle you will need to install a plugin or a device like Creator of Slide Show of the Twinkle of the 3D. There are others that you can use.

The #4 Track Using Google Analytics
The system's offers Facebook Analytics only they limited information, but that is not a problem because you can use in your commercial page Facebook to Google Analytics. Create a new account Google Analytics to use with your URL Facebook. Then copy the number UA supply it and put it into your code of the page.

Application softwares using the Facebook Platform can come over the data of Keen Understandings using the API of the Graph and FQL. You should give permission to let him third-party analytics's software to agree to the data of Keen Understandings for your account.

The Pop #5 Ups
If you find than your page Facebook is you please very important person, you can merge some thereof below the soda above boxes inserting the correct soda above code.

HOW BRINGING UP YOUR FACEBOOK PAGE LIKES

In order that you enjoy the cash Facebook commercializing it you should have an audience. That has importance without the agreement easy to wiggle out of's big base you are a little as talking a room that is empty. You would waste your time. You need to be proactive in order to build the agreement easy to wiggle out of's that big base and to enjoy of the correct marketing Facebook. Having Gustos is the first step in bringing a casual audience over to an agreement easy to wiggle out of and eventually a lover that pays. Let's consider the outstanding pieces of advice of the building of the agreement easy to wiggle out of to you you can implement.

#1's Devices Use Social Plug Ins and of the Taxi Stand Web
Install social ins of the stopper like Facebook Como Caja or Wibiya Toolbar in its place Web or take his personal daily newspaper in the Internet, which one his visits let somebody Taste their page themselves Facebook well of his taxi stand Web. There Web is many other ins of the stopper that you can install easily for your taxi stand's back.

The #2, Create A Gated to you APP Analogous
You he can supply valuable contents using an application software that he requires that you visit Like Them his page before they can come over their contents. How this works you are in reality easy. The application software supplies an image along with a message that it gives you to the visit instructions of

doing click to see the contents in its page like.

The #3's Ads of Commitment
The majority of marketers see publicity ads Facebook like a form to encourage the users to buy something. The ads of commitment are different because they take aim to commercialize their Facebook Page rather promoting the sale of a certain product.

The #4 Get Your Existing Opens Out To Share Its Facebook itself Page Content
His present-day agreement easy to wiggle outs of are key for their building his agreement easy to wiggle out of's base and observing her growing. When you publish contained pertinent in your page, your existent agreement easy to wiggle outs of have a better chance of sharing than the material and that can lead to the new agreement easy to wiggle outs of finding my way to its taxi stand. Placing at sight to this date information also regularly helps to cheer on his fans in order to share the contents that you mail.

The signatures of the E-Mail of the #5
An overlooked form to develop the agreement easy to wiggle outs of to your Facebook Page should often include a signature of the e-mail in all its e-mails. It is easy to implement and very cash. If you not only that business, every day you send a postal number outside electronic and that way having the link for your social taxi stands of networking in your e-mails you promote your growth.

These 5 pieces of advice are a great location to start with to bring up Likes to their Facebook and that way your agreement easy to wiggle out of's base. As your agreement easy to wiggle outs of grow and they share in their contents with their friends, those who then they share their contents with their friends, you will see your reach increasing and with that your agreement easy to wiggle out of's base.

THE TRICKS TO BRING UP YOUR FACEBOOK PAGE LIKES

Your intention is bringing up Likes to its Facebook Page, which means that your agreement easy to wiggle outs of grow. Let's consider some tricks to bring up your Facebook Page Likes and to get benefits.

The #1 of Trick Presented Pleasures
You can exhibit as many as 5 'the Outstanding Pleasures.' These are Pages that you are pleasing for his Page in his Facebook Page. Another excellent technique to use is asking its Featured He Likes To give back the favor for you. This gives you a small fall of publicity.

The marketing Growth of the #2 of Trick
Add everything your marketing opportunities like letterhead, the business cards, the brochures to your URL Facebook, etcetera. Make sure that you destine Facebook to a custom-made URL for your page, because the assigned URLs are for a long time and ugly.

Safe The Check Mark of the #3 of Trick You the offer the Valuable Contents
If you want your fans to visit their page often and share it, back then you need to make sure that you offer contents that is of value. If you consistently decide contained of first class, your agreement easy to wiggle out of that the base will develop as your reach grows. Besides, the first time that somebody finds

his page they will like what they see and they want to read more than what you have to make an offer and so they are a lot more probable for Gustarles your page.

The #4 of Trick, Create A Newsletter to you
If you no longer the step has taken long to create a newsletter to have authority outside for its customers and agreement easy to wiggle outs of, then now it is what's perfect time to make that just. MailChimp along with other suppliers supplies a solution give-away of the newsletter. You can also post in your Facebook Page when your newsletter is available. He does a nice job and supply valuable contents that way it is than that his agreement easy to wiggle outs of he departs that he and you grow his agreement easy to wiggle out of's base.

The #5 of Trick, Create A Facebook to you Calendar
Planning is important and could have planned in advance what you he wants to post about helps you to program and to organize his themes. This creates an environment where you can link themes so that etc is happening in the community, on line, etc back then you can create valuable material that even more earn caning for his 'good timing.'

That is that – 5 big tricks to help you to bring up Likes to your Facebook Page and the agreement easy to wiggle outs of. Keep on many pieces of advice and tricks that 5 can be of value, except the beginning with these easy and they enjoy the benefits. Remember in order that your Facebook Page is a hit you need to develop your agreement easy to wiggle outs of, so give him wings and take care of it!

HOW YOU CAN GROW YOU YOUR FACEBOOK LIKES IN YOUR BUSINESS PAGE

You have created your Facebook Page but without Gustos and agreement easy to wiggle outs of, your page does not go to benefit him the form to her that you want her. Let's look at how you can grow you your pleasures Facebook in your commercial page.

Use Google Analytics to measure ROI. to your Facebook If you have electronic commerce in your taxi stand Web, only you take a little bit of code for you may track your the media's activity social.
Mark your application softwares in order that they have the look and feel of the branding of their company and so they fit with their cover's image. With the exception of foreseen application softwares Facebook (the notes, Events, Pleasures, Photos) you can change the image to equip your branding.
Create the application software's custom buttons. Use a taxi stand like Pixlr.com to check your image for the correct size or even you would be able to have software in his computer to you. You will want your image to be 74 pixels tall for 111 broad pixels to hold the correct proportion.
When you commercialize in Facebook, you should focus on an intention at the same time. Continuing more than what an intention at the same time actually leads to a reduction in its impact.

In your Facebook commercializing, you can help to think as you are the editor of a magazine. Why is the competitor's magazine better than its magazine? How are you going to maintain your hired visit? How are you going to weigh your ads against your contents?

The various select poles to present in their timeline flow. Make the visible pole in your main timeline going to the recent poles for other ones and then gravitating on the correct corner kick of the pole that you have the desire to add your click of the timeline in the X to on and then make a choice 'Allow in Page.'

Have enhanced notifications Facebook Page. You will not lose any poles over there. The system of notification Facebook does not seem to notify the users of comments in for a long time advance with leaden feet so much to make sure you, do not disregard on any use of notifications a third application software of party like the hyper-alerts to maintain him in the loop.

If you are new for Facebook Pages, you can take it outside the Internet until you are pleased with the look and feel of your page. You kept on in order to do this push for your Admin Panel then to choose Edit Page

'Manage Permissions.' Check the box to the side of 'despublique the page.' Then save your changes.

Use Facebook Offers To Bring Up Your Facebook Page Likes

Your Facebook Page's main intention is developing your pleasures and its agreement easy to wiggle outs of aimed at specific areas. A form to do that is taking advantage of Facebook Offers. With offers Facebook, you can share a discount with your audience posting an offer in your Facebook Page.

HOW DESIGNING A FACEBOOK SUCCESSFULLY OFFER

To do your offer is sure claimed as well as shared, you should consider the headline and the image that you use along with the value of the offer. Remember, if people fail to understand that your offer is, would be able to think your unsolicited massive emailing and they would be able to merge you of their Newsworthy Pienso or unlike their Page. That is not what you want to have verificatively, so you do sure your offer it is clear.

There is no minimal value or the discount was necessary you to create an offer Facebook. However, 20 %'s discounts or more will usually catch up with the greater part of people, and it works better than to offer a discount to give something as a present free usually.

How do We Populate Decoy Bird My Offer?

Your visit simply gives a click on Oferta Get and an e-mail will be then it will be sent to them. The person then will need to print the e-mail and to get it into your business to redeem you for whatever the offer went. You should make sure all your staff you are in the know of the Facebook Offers that you run and that they know how to honor and processing these offers, you will in another way have the unhappy customers, who will hurry up to share your bad experience with your friends.

How Creating A Facebook Offer

You should have at least 50 pleasures to take advantage of Facebook Offers. The steps that you need to obey in creating your offer are here.

In his the push of Facebook Page's Timeline for the participative tool. Click Oferta's, Acontecimiento's + and back then give a click on Offer.

Complement everything of the details about his offer. This includes his Headline, TV sending his image, adding up an expiration date, and choosing your audience. You will also establish your budget.

Give a click on them More Alternative and he adds up his starting date, his terms and his conditions, and his on-line redemption.

See in advance than your offer and when you are liked click 'the offer of the Pole.'

There you have it. It is so easy like these four steps creating his Facebook Offer and to begin to enjoy the increasing benefits of both your Pleasures and bringing potentially the new customers at your store. It is one beneficial to both parties all the way round!

4 FORMS THAT YOU CAN INCREASE YOUR FACEBOOK PAGE LIKES

To increase Pleasures to your Facebook is how it increases you your agreement easy to wiggle outs of. The gathering agreement easy to wiggle outs of can be done quickly using a number of tools, but the problem is you want to put all together authentic agreement easy to wiggle outs of that have the potential of the that to become customers instead of simply a bunch 'Pleasures.' Let's look at ourselves in 4 forms that you can enlarge your Facebook Page Gustos with those that they can really build their business.

The #1 Competes and Promotional Contest
It is very easy to run a competition or promotional contest in Facebook. You even can require that
Candidates Facebook have than first becoming an agreement easy to wiggle out of tasting your page to introduce the competition. This can really increase pleasures to his fondness. However, a lot of business undertake that the wrong way. They promote their competition using Newsfeeds. You he should not make this because he goes against Facebook's terms and conditions. Fire your competition correctly using an application software like Wildfire or Strutta. There is a number of other application softwares of competition that you can use. The common guys of competition include submissions of the video

or of the photo. This competition and this method sweepstake they work better when you have on 500 agreement easy to wiggle outs of.

The comment of the #2 in Other Ones Business Pages
If you want to obtain more agreement easy to wiggle outs of Facebook back then you should make you need your page to be so visible as you can possibly get through to a pertinent audience. If you it is a business of the local and mortar brick, you Should Like other local pages. Make comments in his pages like his page and not like his personal name. If you comment on poles where the other ones already have made comments, at the mercy of their adjustments, they will be notified that you posted to give him enlarged visibility.

The #3 of Your Personal Profile Add A Link for Your Business Page
Use your personal profile to add a link to your commercial page. Some of your friends will find what you make useful. You even can mention your page in your bringing ups to date of status now and then to encourage the friends to visit your Page and if they like that you have to make an offer, they would be able to make click the Como button and they would be able to develop their agreement easy to wiggle outs of.

The #4 Friends Invite for like Your Page
You can really give an encouragement to your agreement easy to wiggle out of's base for simply asking you for your friends To Like your page. Make this directly of your page, where you can invite the friends. It is easy and highly effective.

There you he has it – 4 forms to increase his pleasures Facebook Page and consequently his agreement easy to wiggle outs of.